The

Michelangelo

Method

The

Michelangelo

Method

Release Your Inner Masterpiece and Create an Extraordinary Life

KENNETH SCHUMAN AND RONALD PAXTON

New York   Chicago   San Francisco   Lisbon   London   Madrid   Mexico City
Milan   New Delhi   San Juan   Seoul   Singapore   Sydney   Toronto

The *McGraw·Hill* Companies

Library of Congress Cataloging-in-Publication Data

Schuman, Kenneth.
   The Michelangelo method : release your inner masterpiece and create an
extraordinary life / Kenneth Schuman and Ronald Paxton.
         p.   cm.
   Includes bibliographical references.
   ISBN 0-07-147738-1 (alk. paper)
   1. Life skills.   2. Self-help techniques.   I. Paxton, Ronald.   II. Title.

   HQ2037.S27   2007
   158.1—dc22   2006027121

1 2 3 4 5 6 7 8 9 10 11 12 13 14 15   DOC/DOC   0 9 8 7 6

ISBN-13: 978-0-07-147738-3
ISBN-10:   0-07-147738-1

McGraw-Hill books are available at special quantity discounts to use as premiums
and sales promotions, or for use in corporate training programs. For more information,
please write to the Director of Special Sales, Professional Publishing, McGraw-Hill, Two
Penn Plaza, New York, NY 10121-2298. Or contact your local bookstore.

This book is printed on acid-free paper.

To my wife, Wendy, who has always been my soul's partner and will always be my greatest love. To my children, Cory and Andy, who fill my heart with joy and give my life its ultimate meaning.

—Kenneth Schuman

To my wife, Nancy, who introduced me to the integrity and magnificence of Michelangelo's masterpieces four decades ago, for sharing her life and love with me. To my children, Jill and Brad, who inspire me with their steadfast commitment to their life dreams. To my coaches, Susan Wallace and David Burnet, who guided and supported me as I found my way to a life that fits me. To my clients, who have honored me and taught me, by inviting me to stand for them on their journey to an extraordinary life.

—Ronald Paxton

Contents

Acknowledgments

Writing this book has been a joyful journey, from the point three years ago when we decided that we had a message we wanted to convey to the point at which we created the final manuscript for *The Michelangelo Method*. We would like to thank those who have guided us along this new and challenging path.

First and foremost we would like to thank Wendy Schuman, who has participated in all stages of the development of the book, providing invaluable assistance in shaping and refining it through her insights and skills in writing and editing.

Special thanks to Jason Tarantino, who helped us create an engaging narrative style that brought the case studies to life.

We would like to thank Joelle Delbourgo, our agent, for recognizing the book's potential and for her fine work in finding just the right publisher.

We are extremely grateful to Deborah Brody, senior editor at McGraw-Hill, for the vision, guidance, and practical help that she has provided in bringing this work to its current form.

Finally, we would like to thank our clients, who allowed us to share their inspiring stories to illustrate the principles of the Michelangelo Method.

Bust of Michelangelo by da Volterra
Daniele da Volterra created this bust from Michelangelo's
death mask shortly after Michelangelo's death in 1564.
Photograph by Ken Schuman

Introduction

Without having seen the Sistine Chapel one can form no appreciable idea of what one man is capable of achieving.
—Johann Wolfgang von Goethe,
Rome, 1787 (written after viewing
Michelangelo's magnificent paintings
in fresco, including more than three
hundred figures and covering nearly
six thousand square feet of the
Vatican's Sistine Chapel ceiling)

You can find masters working in an endless array of fields—in art; in science; in government; in business; in sales and marketing; in engineering; in photography, cooking, dancing, singing, and acting; in accounting—in any activity that people devote their lives to with relish. There are at least a few thousand masters, maybe more, in every field. That's a shocking statement!

And not throughout history, but right now. To think that mastery of a field isn't some rare event that occurs only every other century when the moon is blue. To think that mastery is possible, not just for names scrawled in the musty pages of history, but for all of us. It is. Right now, mastery is living inside all of us.

Inside of you. In fact, your masterpiece is already there, just waiting to be revealed. To understand what that masterpiece is, you simply need the vision to see inside yourself, to understand the personal values, passions, and talents that will lead you to its expression.

>>> *Right now, mastery is living inside all of us.* <<<

Michelangelo Buonarroti

While there have been countless masters throughout history, there exist very, very few who have truly mastered more than one field.

Anton Chekhov, a master playwright and author, was a thriving country doctor. Thomas Jefferson was both a brilliant statesman and an architect. Leonardo da Vinci, the great painter, was also an inventor whose wondrous discoveries were years ahead of their time. Such masters of two fields are extremely rare.

There is, however, one person in history who inarguably achieved mastery in three different fields: Michelangelo Buonarroti. In each of the fields he pursued—sculpture, painting, and architecture—

Michelangelo created and innovated, forging a path for future practitioners to follow. Whether it was in the detailed strokes and complex iconography of the Sistine Chapel, the impossible chisel strikes that yielded the superb anatomy of his *David*, or the magnificent dome of St. Peter's Basilica, Michelangelo demonstrated mastery of his craft.

⇛ *Discover your personal path to mastery.* ⇚

There are valuable lessons to be learned from the life of Michelangelo and the way he approached his work and life—lessons that, when applied to our lives, enable powerful breakthroughs that reveal our personal path to mastery.

The book you hold in your hands, *The Michelangelo Method*, unveils these strategies and provides real-life lessons in applying them to design an extraordinary life that works for you.

The strategies described in this book are drawn directly from Michelangelo's actual life and work, which were remarkably well documented by his own writings (he was a prolific letter writer and poet) and firsthand accounts of his contemporary biographers, Giorgio Vasari and Ascanio Condivi, as well as later authors.

This book, while written by two different coaches, is told from the perspective of a single coaching persona. This eliminates the irksome problem of repeatedly having to distinguish which of the experiences relate to which author—"I, Kenneth Schuman," or "I, Ronald Paxton." Both of the authors subscribe wholeheartedly to the method and coaching approach provided in this book and, as such, really do speak with a single voice.

This book contains twelve case studies that demonstrate how the Michelangelo Method can inspire, guide, and support you through difficult career and life transformations. Each of these case histories is based on a real coaching client, though the names and some of the identifying details have been changed for privacy. We believe you'll see something in these stories that relates to your situation as you apply the coaching and insights to releasing your own inner masterpiece.

You'll learn how to do the following:

+ Identify your personal masterpiece already within you, just as Michelangelo envisioned his *David* within a huge slab of uncut stone.

+ Find your unique purpose by connecting your strengths, passions, and values.

+ Build on your strengths to develop the talents and abilities necessary to achieve your vision.

+ Commit to your vision with the confidence needed to achieve success.

+ Remove the internal and external blocks that hold you back.

+ Develop the supportive network necessary for you to discover and pursue your vision.

+ Fight for your vision by gathering your energy and resources to overcome obstacles.

+ Push your limits and take appropriate risks to create your personal masterpiece.

+ Creatively connect and blend your life experiences to allow you to master new challenges.

We invite you to begin to create your own extraordinary life using the empowering questions and discovery exercises included in each chapter, the resources provided in the Appendices, and additional resources available on our website, michelangelomethod.com. The Michelangelo Method will empower you to create a life that fits and energizes you while fulfilling your unique purpose.

David

Michelangelo sought to create a statue that would rally the
Republic of Florence against its more powerful enemies
using a "gigantic, ruined" block of marble. Michelangelo
stated that, as David had conquered his Goliath in the flesh
with his sling, Michelangelo would overcome his giant in
marble with his carving tools.

Photograph by Ron Paxton

1
....
Envision Your
Masterpiece Within

The greatest artist has no conception which a single block of marble does not potentially contain within its mass, but only a hand obedient to the mind can penetrate to this image.
—Michelangelo Buonarroti

The Image Inside the Stone

Sculpture is a daunting art form. Just imagine an immense hunk of rock, tons of weight straining the floorboards of your artist's studio. Now imagine yourself before that rock. The rock dwarfs you. Resting before you, it stands as an impenetrable, immovable giant. Now imagine you're to begin sculpting a commission for the church, a powerful family, or perhaps the rulers of the land.

How are you to turn this rock into a wondrous Pietà?

And even if you begin to have some success and your vision starts to take form, one false move with that chisel, one slight slip of that hammer—or even one fault line in the rock that you hadn't anticipated—and in just one second your work may be damaged beyond repair. So imagine sculpting Michelangelo's *David*, the embodiment of a young hero standing more than fourteen feet tall. Imagine the challenge of setting out to create one of the greatest masterpieces of sculpture in the history of humankind.

There is little doubt that Michelangelo was one of history's greatest sculptors, a man who could transform a solid block of marble into a lifelike form that married Greek and Roman proportion and technique with a passionate expressionism that had never been seen before in the art form. But even considering his genius, just how in the world did Michelangelo sculpt the *David* from a giant block of stone so damaged that his contemporaries considered it "ruined" and "a thing of no value"? What was it that allowed Michelangelo to succeed in the face of this challenge? How did he even begin?

The answer is simple. Michelangelo looked at the block and saw his *David* locked inside.

Michelangelo held an important belief about the art of sculpture. He believed that in each block of stone there was a figure hidden inside, waiting to be revealed. To Michelangelo, the master sculptor's job was clear: chip away what is not the figure and reveal the masterpiece inside the stone. As Michelangelo described the process in one of his sonnets:

> With chiseled touch
> The stone unhewn and cold
> Becomes a living mould.
> The more the marble wastes,
> The more the statue grows.

With this perspective, the task of extracting a *David* from bedrock is less daunting. *David* is already there. It was simply Michelangelo's job to reveal him.

⇢ *Inside of you there is a David.* ⇠

Whoever you are, whatever you are doing, inside the stone of your ordinary life, there is a masterpiece. To uncover that masterpiece hidden inside the life you're living now, to achieve the breakthroughs you want in your career and in your life, you, like Michelangelo, must see that it is already there. You must look within yourself. You must heed what you truly value, harness your passions, and envision the masterpiece that's inside.

Ben

When I first met him, Ben looked every bit the part of a master of the universe—a high-powered, New York City investment banker. The dark blue suit, the red tie, the bonus checks, the multimillion-dollar deals, the rushed words on the phone, the hurried look, the setting of appointments in his day planner—one overlapping the other—Ben's image was rock solid.

This was, after all, who Ben was. Just more than a year earlier, Ben's mentor had offered him a position at a prestigious Manhattan-based investment bank in corporate finance. And Ben, talented and smart, easily made the transition from his career in state government, where he had been serving as development commissioner, to investment banking. If Ben continued to prove successful in his new career, he would earn a multimillion-dollar income in only a short period of time. This was a dream job, and it was one that was also well suited to Ben's abilities as a businessman, a manager, and an influencer. While on the surface Ben appeared comfortable in his investment banking role, inside there was another Ben. And this Ben was cramped and uneasy.

From deep inside this investment banker shell, this other Ben watched his life change. The banker suit and tie went on. The eighty-plus-hour workweek replaced the hours spent with his wife and his daughter. The future shifted, and not just in terms of his finances, but in terms of his family.

Working late at night in the brightly lit office, Ben found himself in conversations with his colleagues over takeout Chinese food. His colleagues' stories were always the same: the problems they were having with their wives or their second wives, how their wives wanted them to spend more time with the kids, the anniversary dinners they missed when term sheets had to be changed for the mergers they were working on.

And oh, his colleagues' laments! Couldn't their wives understand that if they wanted the money and the lifestyle that went along with it—the personal chef, the house in the Hamptons, the Chanel and the Gucci, the private schools—if they wanted all that this work afforded them, then they would have to make a small sacrifice? And besides, they would complain, "Can't they see I love what I do?"

Ben began to compare his life with the lives of his colleagues. Many of his most successful colleagues seemed to enjoy spending time with their work more than they did with their wives and families. Did Ben?

Sometimes late at night, when stuck in a particularly thorny financial model, Ben would sit at his desk and stare at the pictures he kept upon it. He would fix on the image of his nine-year-old daughter. She stood there in the living room of his apartment, smiling at him through the space of the camera lens and time. Dressed in a frilly pink tutu, she had her arms raised high above her head, and her feet were settled somewhat awkwardly in first position. He thought of his wife on the other side of the camera, alone in their apartment, snapping a picture for her absent husband.

Ben looked back at the complex jumble of the spreadsheet. The numbers didn't add up. Ben no longer equaled Ben.

⟫ *Crises rarely come at convenient times.* ⟪

One wintry January evening, with snow falling harder and harder outside, his wife out of town on an assignment for a magazine article, his daughter at home with a babysitter, there, downtown in the heart of Wall Street, Ben waited for word from a senior partner about a big deal that was about to come down. Ben was supposed to be home at 6 P.M. to relieve the babysitter. With the blizzard, one would have assumed Ben would head home even earlier. Big deals, however, do not stop for blizzards, time, or other acts of God.

It was 5 P.M. when the papers finally came through and fell onto Ben's desk in a mess of figures for his expert analysis. Millions of dollars were on the line. Hours of work in preparing his report lay ahead. The snow kept coming down, inches already on the ground.

The phone rang in Ben's office at 7 P.M. The babysitter had already stayed longer than she had agreed to. Her voice betrayed her panic and annoyance. This was to be the biggest storm of the year, she told him. "The weatherman said everyone needs to get home, and my mom wants me home now."

Ben was at a loss. His wife was hundreds of miles away, his babysitter had to leave, and he was stuck at work. This was quite a dilemma. His family needed him; his work needed him. Ben needed to make a choice.

In scooping the papers up into his briefcase, flying down the stairs, hopping in a cab, and making the slippery journey uptown to his home, Ben made his choice. He chose his family.

In that cab ride home, Ben, for perhaps the first time, saw a glimpse inside the stone. A crack had opened in the investment banker facade that he had been carefully polishing, and inside he saw himself cramped and compromised.

When Ben opened the door of his home, his daughter rushed at him, her arms wide. "It's snowing, Daddy." She jumped into his arms. As he held her, inside Ben felt his inner self stretch and push the cramped space out.

>>> *The key to your masterpiece is found in your values and passions.* <<<

When Ben came to see me, we both knew that for him change was imminent; he was just unsure what that change should be. Ben knew he had potential. He had been told that time and time again, by his mentor, his coworkers, his bosses, his family, his friends. Ben believed what they said was true—if he applied himself, he could create a masterpiece. He just couldn't fathom what it was.

Ben had started to worry. Maybe everything he had been told was wrong. Maybe he wasn't meant to be a master of anything.

Maybe he was meant to fall short, a man whose promise never materialized.

What Ben didn't know was that the vision for his masterpiece was already inside him. He just needed to see it, his *David* inside the block of stone.

To envision his masterpiece, Ben needed to understand only two things. First, what did Ben truly value in life? Second, what were his passions?

When we initially sat and spoke, I asked Ben what thoughts first drifted through his mind when he didn't have anything else he was supposed to be thinking about. His answer was profoundly clear. "My wife and daughter. Always." There was no question. Clearly, one of the most important values in Ben's life was maintaining his family. If he were going to break through to his masterpiece, he would need to align his career with his values. He would need to strike a balance between his work and his family life.

But Ben's valuing of family was just one piece of the puzzle. A value is what you hold dear. It's what you believe to be important; it's what you should never disavow. But it's not something you *do*; it is not a driving force. A value is a way of being, not doing. The driving force, that doing, is your passion. A passion is what you would do if you had unlimited resources and time; it's what you dreamed of doing when you were growing up; it's the engine that takes you to your masterpiece.

⇢ *A passion is what you are driven to do.* ⇠

When I looked at Ben's career history, his passions came into focus. Talking to Ben, I learned that he came out of school with an M.B.A. during the height of the Vietnam era. But unlike others who had used their M.B.A. to rapidly ascend the corporate ladder, Ben took a different path. After graduate school Ben promptly became a teacher in the rough schools of the South Bronx. While altruism wasn't his only motivation—during the Vietnam War, teaching in a city school offered a draft deferment—teaching opened his eyes to the difference a person could make, especially in an area as troubled as the South Bronx in the early 1970s.

After managing the challenges of teaching in this difficult environment, Ben decided that he could use his M.B.A. to make a difference. He looked for a job in New York's not-for-profit world. Ben found himself running a center that helped high-risk families navigate the city's complex social program infrastructure, avoiding the need to place the children into foster care.

I asked Ben to tell me a little about his work at the center. His eyes widened. I could see a fire glowing inside him. "The stories I could tell you."

We were onto something.

⇛ *Find work that ignites a fire inside you.* ⇚

"OK. This is what it was like doing that work. You see, the center I ran had a number of different offices that represented the various high-risk neighborhoods in New York City. I had the opportunity to work at each of them, but at one point, I spent some time heading up our office in Chinatown.

"One day, a Vietnamese woman walked into our office with her three children. She spoke no English, and as our Chinese-speaking workers were not fluent in Vietnamese, communication was challenging, to say the least. But we didn't need to understand her language to comprehend that she was in desperate straits. Tears were in her eyes as she attempted to relate her story to our team. Working together, we managed to find a common language—some French, a few phrases of Vietnamese, a little Mandarin—and soon we learned her story.

"She was about thirty and had only recently arrived in the United States from Saigon. Of course, this was during the final days of the Vietnam War, and you can only imagine the chaos and bloodshed that this woman had seen. Well, somehow in the middle of that chaos, her husband had put her and her children on a boat and sent them off to the United States with their family savings and a promise that he would follow them just a few weeks later.

"Weeks passed, and her husband did not arrive. Fearing the worst, she began to search for word of his fate. Through personal networks—assorted family members on garbled long-distance calls, distant cousins, relatives of others who had come over from Vietnam—she learned that the worst had come true. Her husband was dead—just another civilian casualty of the war.

"Now, here she was in a strange city, coping with this loss, attempting to find a job—which proved to be difficult because she was unable to speak English—and dealing with her family. And the latter was becoming more difficult with each passing day.

"Her youngest son had severe asthma—you could literally hear his wheezing the moment they walked into the office. And the conditions they were living in—a dirty, small apartment with two other families—were not ideal for nursing him to health. Her middle son, once a model child, was acting out. Clearly traumatized by the horror he had witnessed in Saigon and by the loss of his father, he had become a severe discipline problem, constantly mouthing off to his mother and fighting with his younger brother. Her eldest was perhaps the worst problem of all. A former honors student in Vietnam, he was now lost in the public school system. Lacking adequate English skills, he was failing his classes. And worse, he was hanging out after school with one of the many gangs on the streets of Chinatown. You don't have to be a counselor to understand that this family was truly in trouble.

"Seeing someone who had suffered so much and who was clearly struggling to keep things together—well, you just want to help. And fortunately we were able to. Our team went into action. We recruited a native Vietnamese speaker. We enrolled the woman in an English as a second language program. We found her a part-time job cleaning houses for neighbors in the Chinatown community. We found mental health support for her two troubled children and medical help for her asthmatic child. We helped her navigate welfare. We helped her get public housing. We enrolled her children in tutoring and after-school programs that kept them off the streets while she worked. We did everything we could to help keep their family together.

"And after two years passed, I was able to close her file, a success. Her youngest son's health had improved dramatically. Her middle child began to take interest in sports—he excelled in track—and he recovered the discipline he had in Vietnam. And her eldest son rediscovered his love of science and found himself excelling enough in the local public school to gain entrance in his junior year to the prestigious program at the Bronx High School of Science. As for the woman, with her improved language skills, she managed to find stable work that allowed her to begin to put away money for her sons' college education. It was a truly amazing success."

Ben paused for a long moment, clearly holding that image from his past in his mind. And then he laughed, shaking off the power of his own feeling. "I guess, that's a long way of saying, that's what it was like."

⟫⟫ *Dig beneath your facade to find your true self.* ⟪⟪

After hearing him tell his story, I clearly saw that Ben's passion was helping people. No wonder he found it so difficult to work in a field like investment banking, a field where the focus is solely financial.

The fact was that if Ben was not helping people, he was not truly being Ben. Regardless of the suit and tie and the busy calendar, deep down, behind the strong facade was his real masterpiece, which involved working with his passions in a way that fit with what he valued in life. Ben just needed to see it inside the stone.

Ben would need to start by doing two things. First, he would need to recognize that his core value was his family, and he would need to find a career that would allow him to spend quality time with them. Second, he would need to find a career that would allow him to truly follow his passion, helping others.

Later, Ben would find an opportunity that would help him to break through to that vision and uncover the truest expression of his self. The work wouldn't be easy—sculpture is as hard as stone—but after he'd taken the right first step, there was no doubt that in the end, Ben's work would lead to one thing: a masterpiece.

Sculpt Your Personal Masterpiece

Michelangelo held an important belief about the art of sculpture: he beheld a slab of marble and saw the figure within, struggling to be released.

Whatever your situation, no matter how hard change seems, hidden inside the stone of your day-to-day life there is a masterpiece. To release that masterpiece, to achieve the breakthroughs that will lead you to an extraordinary life and career, you must look deep within yourself; develop a vision of your life that aligns your values, passions, and talents; and then, from that vision, create your masterpiece.

If you are ready to make the breakthrough to your extraordinary life, then do what Ben did. Home in on your personal values and unlock your passions. Create the foundation you need to see the masterpiece that's inside you.

Discover Your Personal Values

A value is what you believe in, what you consider worthwhile or desirable. Having a life that includes your leading values is of fundamental importance to your personal happiness. Achievement, adventure, beauty, creativity, power, love, loyalty, religion, friendship, knowledge—all of these are examples of personal values. The question is, what do you value in your life?

Extracting your personal values requires that you ask yourself some important and difficult questions:

+ Who are my role models in life, and what qualities do I admire them for?

+ How do I spend my leisure time?

+ What is the feeling that I get when I am doing that leisure-time activity?

+ If I had more money than I could ever spend, what would I do with my time?

+ What feeling might I have while doing that activity?

+ What energizes me at work?

Once you have some preliminary thoughts in mind, talk about your values with someone who knows you well and confirm with that person that you're on the right track. No need to debate—just consider the responses as additional input.

(Discovery Exercises

1. Write down answers to each of the preceding questions, and extract all the personal values encompassed by those activities. Try to pinpoint exactly what it is that you value. For instance, if you spend your leisure time exercising, is it beauty or health that you value the most? Or perhaps you value your gym time as a way to socialize with others. Consider other choices that you make in your life. Are you more excited about the organic grocery that was built in your town or the new cosmetics store? If the answer is the organic grocery, perhaps you value health above all else.

2. Refer to the list of personal values in Appendix A. Select the five values you can relate to the best (adding any you may think of). Write these five values on individual three-by-five index cards.

3. Study the five index cards. If you absolutely had to lose one of these values from your life, which would you give up? When you've truly decided which value you can live without, remove that card. Repeat this process until you have two cards left. These are your two most important personal values. Be sure that these values are incorporated into your life in some important way. Look for ways to include your other key values as well.

Unlock Your Passions

A passion is the engine that drives you to your masterpiece. It's something you do that gives you great joy and engages your deepest emotions. It's not just what you do; it's what you choose to do. See Appendix A for a list of sample passions. Create your own unique list of your passions.

To unlock your passions, ask yourself the following questions:

+ When I wake up in the morning, what do I look forward to?

+ As my mind wanders throughout the day, what do I daydream about?

+ What activities do I wish I could do in the middle of my workday?

+ What hobbies do I keep up with?

+ What did I want to be "when I grew up"?

+ What or whom do I like to read about?

+ What do I like to talk about with friends and family?

Your answers to these questions will reveal what you are truly passionate about. Perhaps you spend your leisure time trying to save an endangered forest. Clearly, you are passionate about the environment and making the planet a better place for people to live. Maybe you enjoy nothing more than restoring old cars. Or you might be passionate about learning how things work or about craftsmanship.

Talk to the people closest to you. Share with them your thoughts on your passions. See if they echo your thinking.

Discovery Exercises

1. List as many activities as you can that relate to the preceding seven questions.

2. See which activities come up more than once. What themes do you see? For instance, if you listed "traveling" under wishes, hobbies, and what you like to talk about, it's a pretty good bet that this is one of your greatest passions. (Michelangelo's overriding passion was sculpting. Even while painting the ceiling of the Sistine Chapel, he still considered himself to be a sculptor.)

3. Check your passions against the values you uncovered in the previous exercise. If your passion is travel, perhaps one of your highest values is adventure or knowledge. Values and passions that reinforce each other are much stronger and more lasting.

Captive Called Atlas

Michelangelo believed that the figure he was seeking to carve was imprisoned in the stone and he was gradually releasing it. First, he outlined the figure on the front of the block. Then he chipped away from one side, working into the stone. As parts of the body emerged, his vision came into focus.

2

Discover Your Gift

While Michelangelo was having the tomb of Julius II finished, he gave directions to a stone-cutter: "Cut away this today, smooth out in this place, and polish up in that." In the course of time, without being aware of it, the man found that he had produced a statue, and stared astonished at his own performance. Michelangelo asked, "What do you think of it?" "I think it very good," he answered, "and I owe you a deep debt of gratitude." "Why do you say that?" asked Michelangelo. "Because you have caused me to discover in myself a talent which I did not know that I possessed."

—Life of Michelangelo,
Giorgio Vasari, 1568

Michelangelo's Gift

We find our own personal masterpieces by understanding where our values, passions, and strengths intersect. From this very powerful nexus we can sculpt the life we really want. Michelangelo found this intersection in his own life. His strength from an early age was in drafting, transferring to paper what his eyes saw or his mind imagined. He knew this and nurtured it by drawing whenever he had the chance. In the words of his contemporary Giorgio Vasari, "Since Michelangelo's genius drew him to delight in design, all the time he could snatch he would spend in drawing in secret, being scolded for this by his father and other elders, and at times beaten." Michelangelo expressed the belief that drawing was the source from which flowed the rivers of painting, sculpture, and architecture.

With training in the workshop of Domenico Ghirlandaio and at the Medici artists' school, Michelangelo further developed his talent in drawing and developed his lifelong passion for sculpture.

But for Michelangelo's strengths and passions to be truly transformed into his gift, they had to become aligned with his values. Michelangelo's chief value—what he cared about most—was to glorify God. Michelangelo believed that man was created in God's image and that the soul needs to escape materiality to reconnect with God. He believed that in rendering God's highest creation as perfectly as possible in stone, he was glorifying God. And in his remarkable series of sculptures known as the Captives, the figures seem to be struggling to escape from the stone—a metaphor for the enslavement of the human spirit within the body and the beginning of the soul's journey to God. From his famous *Last Judgment* in the Vatican and his sculptures of David, the Captives, and the three Pietàs, to the soaring dome he designed for St. Peter's Basilica in Rome, he saw his work as the outgrowth of his most deeply held values.

For Michelangelo, connecting his values, passions, and strengths generated the energy and creative spirit needed for each masterpiece. He honed his strength of drafting, which he described as "a hand obedient to the mind," to pursue his passion, sculpting, in the service of his most deeply held value, glorifying God, by depicting the beauty and perfection of man. He found no greater joy than to use this gift, and he was working on his final masterpiece, the *Rondanini Pietà*, the week before his death at age eighty-nine.

Susan

For our first meeting, Susan arrived late, exactly twenty-three minutes late, or so she told me. She would know. Susan's watch was set by satellite.

When Susan hurried into my office, she was dressed in her corporate suit with Nikes on her feet, a symbol of the marathon her life had become. "I am so sorry. But you should have seen the traffic."

Susan, I would come to learn, was terribly frazzled. She had good reason to be. For the past sixteen years, she had been the quintessential single mother, juggling a demanding career and taking care of her daughter without any help from the child's chronically absent father. Deep down Susan was ambitious. To make her life more challenging, she pushed herself over the years to keep more and more balls in the air. Every year, she would take on more work, more community service, and more professional development classes; and she would take her daughter to more extracurricular activities. While Susan was a master juggler, no one could keep up with her performance schedule. And fewer could meet the expectations she set for herself.

Susan was head legal assistant at a major white-shoe law firm. Her daughter, "the flower from my compost heap of a marriage," as she colorfully put it, had recently left for college on an academic scholarship. For the past sixteen years, Susan had seen herself constantly pulled in two directions—trying to care for her daughter and her career—and not meeting her own standards for either. Inside, she was torn with frustration. With her daughter launched and off to college, Susan was left to consider her own path. She looked down at the ground below her. "Dull, poured cement all around," she said, "and my feet were planted in it long before I had a chance to choose."

>> *Choose where to plant your feet.* <<

Susan wanted a change. She was dying for a change. But to what? She had no idea. And wasn't it too late already? Time had passed her by. After all, she was nearly forty-one. Susan couldn't think constructively. She believed that she had no choices. Here was a bright, articulate, capable woman who could do practically anything she set her mind to but who, in her own mind, could never do anything right and had missed her chance anyway.

Susan believed she was a failure. Her life was nothing more than a giant "might have been." If she hadn't married so young, she might have had a relationship she was happy with. If she hadn't gotten pregnant, she might have finished law school. If she had had the chance, she might have been the lawyer and not the legal assistant. In Susan's mind, she wasn't late—she had never had a chance to arrive. Even now, ready to open herself to a new life, Susan couldn't figure out where to begin. But she was committed to finding her way, for her greatest fear was that, as Oliver Wendell Holmes put it, she might be among those "who die with our music still within us." For Susan, it was time to start playing her own music.

"How do I find out what exactly to do? Can you tell me?" Her eyes desperately probed mine for an answer.

"You have to find it within yourself," I replied. "But I can start by asking you a few questions that will begin to reveal your gift."

"But I don't have a particular gift."

Everyone Has a Gift

If you were to ask someone what his or her gift is, chances are that person's mind will immediately turn to Michelangelo sculpting his *Pietà* or Einstein unlocking the universe's secrets with a simple equation or something else equally remarkable. People tend to think of gifts in such extraordinary terms. They see a gift as an innate, exceptional talent, as something that few people in this life are blessed with.

But they are wrong.

The fact is that a gift isn't exclusive to the exceptionally talented, the successful, or the blessed. Quite the contrary—everyone has a gift. Some are a thousand watts of bold light. Others are hidden in the stone. All are there, waiting to be revealed.

You find your gift in the place where your values, passions, and strengths meet. Discovering that place, finding your gift, is the first step toward sculpting your extraordinary life. For if in your life you are not using your own special gift, you will find yourself uncomfortable, dissatisfied, and frustrated with life, much like Susan. Yet if, like Susan, you're looking for your "place in the world," the first thing you must do, before anything else, is to locate the place where your values, passions, and strengths converge.

Susan's Passion

When I started to ask Susan about her passion, I knew I was entering uncharted territory.

I asked, "Susan, when you wake up in the morning, or if your mind wanders during the day, what are you thinking of?"

"Oh, there are lots of crazy thoughts running through my head."

"I really want to know," I encouraged her, "no matter how crazy you think they sound."

After a pause, she said hesitantly, "Sometimes when I'm sitting at my desk I get this picture in my head, this picture of a desolate beach. There are no people, just seagulls that fly down and land on the shoreline. And I'm there. But I'm not doing anything in particular. I'm just walking on the shore and watching the birds: how they do what they do, how they groom themselves, the creatures they go after, the way they react to the water when it floats in too close to them. It's stupid. I don't know why I said it."

"No, that's exactly what we're looking for. Do you spend a lot of your leisure time at the beach?"

"Oh no, not at all. I'd occasionally take my daughter out there when she was younger, and we'd enjoy walking together. But mostly we tended to go to the mountains. I guess the whole thing is less about the beach than it is that I love watching nature. Mostly in this wildlife preserve that's about a half hour from my home. I like to hike and watch how the rabbits, woodchucks, squirrels, and other animals behave."

⇛ Consider why you do what you do. ⇚

"What is it about watching these animals that you like?"

"I don't know exactly. I guess I've adored animals since I was a kid. When I was a little girl, I used to say I was going to be a veterinarian when I grew up. But I really didn't want to be a veterinarian. While I was crazy about animals, I didn't love the thought of operating on them. I was certainly too squeamish for that. But I did love watching spiders build webs on our back porch. Or birds take off in flight. I loved the outdoors. I loved hiking. Still do. But you know, as I'm sitting here thinking about it with you, I guess it's not just about the nature. I love watching people, too. It's part of what I adore about being in the city on my lunch hour—just watching people and how they interact."

"So you're curious about how people interact with their environment."

Her eyes relaxed into a thought. I could see that we were making progress. "Exactly. Yes."

"What is it about their interactions that attract you?"

"I guess it's trying to understand what exactly is going on. Trying to figure out what they're doing and where they're going, trying to predict how they'll act if a certain circumstance is presented. I mean, this is some of what I do in my job. When you're working for someone, you're always trying to guess which way they're apt to move in a given circumstance. And when you're doing that inside the political landscape of a big company—and there are more politics at that level than you could ever imagine—you're not only analyzing their next move, you're looking at everyone else's, too. If you don't, you simply can't do a good job. I guess that's what I'm doing when I look at nature. Of course, watching nature has nothing to do with work."

I nodded. "On one level, yes. But would you say when you're doing your work—or better yet, when you're out in nature and you're watching, say, a spider making its web—are you trying to appreciate the beauty and intricate patterns of the web? Or are you imagining stories about the spider? Or are you more concerned with collecting information about the spider, charting its course—how much it's accomplished? Or is it something else?"

"I guess it's more that I'm trying to figure out what it's doing and what makes it tick."

"You said you studied anthropology when you were first in school," I noted, trying to further explore her interests. "Did you enjoy it?"

"Yes. In fact, I still enjoy reading anthropology journals when I get the chance. I'm just fascinated with people and culture."

"Do you read a lot?"

"Absolutely. I read nature magazines, science journals, and books. And I've tried to instill that love in my daughter. When we're on a hike, I'll take a guidebook around and read about some of the flora and fauna we're coming across. I guess it's not only for her benefit. I just love to learn new things."

"It sounds like you're passionate about learning."

"I hadn't thought of it that way, but I guess now that we're talking about it, yes, you're right." For the first time, I saw Susan smile. "If my daughter were here, she'd say I'm such a nerd."

And there we were. Susan's daughter knew what Susan had never taken the time to understand. Susan loved learning. And if Susan's work was to be aligned with who Susan really was, that work would need to include her passion for learning as a central focus.

But this passion for learning was just a single part of the three-part equation. For Susan to unwrap her gift, she would need to discover her values and strengths as well.

Susan's Values

"Is there anyone you've studied about or met who has left a deep impression on you?" I asked Susan.

"I know it sounds odd, but I would have to say Gandhi. Not for the reasons that you might think, though. It's because he understood who he was and stood up for himself and what he cared about."

"What do you mean?"

"Well, you couldn't push him around. Even though he was little. I mean you could pick him up and throw him, but deep down, where it mattered, he stood his ground. He said what was true, without any pretense, no matter what the consequences. Most people are about looking good. Gandhi couldn't care less about what people thought of him personally. What you saw was what you got. He cared about being true to himself."

"Were you ever pushed around?"

"Are you kidding? All the time. I was the youngest of three girls. My middle sister, Dorothy, was two years older and always on my case. She would torment me by twisting the heads off my dolls or punching my stuffed animals in the face. I had to learn to stand up for myself. I was afraid of her. But I've learned not to let fear rule my life. I'm getting a lot better."

"And Gandhi served as a model for you?"

"He was willing to risk everything to be himself. He risked his life. He risked his family. He was from the spirit, from the soul. He was authentic.

"And authenticity is what you value?

"Well, of course," Susan responded with conviction. "If you can't be who you really are, then you're just pretending to live your life. You have to be able to honestly express what you believe—in your words and actions. Gandhi knew this. He was the genuine article."

Susan's Strengths

Susan's passion was her love of learning, and her chief value was authenticity. The challenge was to find the space where they met. If she could do this, Susan would surely find the spark of inspiration she was looking for in her work. And if she could channel her strengths toward this spark, she could truly begin to make the contribution to the world that she so desperately wanted to make. Finding these strengths was the last part of opening Susan's gift.

Thankfully, Susan's strength was not so difficult to find. She was an unusually observant person. She not only loved observing people, plants, and wildlife, but she was exceptionally good at it. Moreover, all the time she had spent observing the behavior of small animals on her hikes and at the beach and observing people interacting during her lunch breaks had nurtured and sharpened this skill. And it was a skill that Susan had already put to good use in the workplace, enabling her to figure out her boss's needs and to negotiate the complex office politics that confronted her each day.

Once we uncovered this strength, the pieces of Susan's puzzle finally locked together. Susan's strength was her observation skills. Her passion was love of learning. She valued authenticity above all else. Susan would find her gift in a field that involved learning and allowed her to authentically express who she is and that made full use of her observation skills.

In our subsequent meetings Susan and I would begin to uncover various career possibilities. She researched several potential careers. She asked her friends and relatives what they thought she would enjoy doing. Eventually, Susan would find herself embarking on a new career in teaching science to high school students—a career that incorporated studying and teaching biology and chemistry; that permitted her to be honest with herself, her students, and her colleagues; and that required her skills in observation. Her journey to even conceive of that career was, in and of itself, a long road. And when Susan left my office that day, her feet took the first steps on a road she had chosen. She was finally free to begin her journey.

Sculpt Your Personal Masterpiece

We find our personal masterpiece by understanding where our values, passions, and strengths intersect. From this very powerful place we can sculpt the life we really want. But first you need to dig deep within yourself. In Chapter 1 we learned how to discover our personal values and unlock our passions. But unless we combine these with our strengths—in Michelangelo's case, the "hand obedient to the mind"; for Susan, her observation abilities—we will not be able to uncover our gifts and create the extraordinary lives we seek.

Identify Your Strengths

To determine your strengths, write down your answers to the following questions:

+ In what areas do people come to me for advice?

+ What am I best at in my work?

+ What skills do I develop in my spare time?

+ What activities bring me joy simply in doing them?

+ What am I naturally good at?

+ What do I do to relieve stress? (People often turn to what they are good at.)

You can refer to Appendix A for a sample list of strengths to assist you in creating your individual list. Note that passions and strengths can overlap. For example, you may be passionate about photography but are satisfied with simply taking snapshots for friends and family. Or you may be an advanced amateur or professional photographer who is passionate about photography and has mastered skills such as lighting, exposure, portraiture, sports photography, and other advanced creative and technical skills related to photography. Beginners and amateurs may be passionate about photography, and they can, of course, develop advanced skills, but photography would not be a current strength for them.

Discovery Exercises

1. Rate the strengths you provided as answers to the preceding questions in order, with number 1 being your greatest strength, number 2 your second greatest strength, and so on.

2. Find three people who know you well, and ask them to order your list of your strengths based on their understanding of you. Review their answers with them, particularly with regard to the areas of difference with your own answers. Again, no need to debate—simply consider the feedback.

3. Revisit your list in view of the feedback you have received. Make revisions to the ordering of your strengths as you feel appropriate.

Align Your Values, Passions, and Strengths

Once you've identified your strengths, look for where they intersect with your values and passions. Make this connection, and you will be able to generate enormous power. Do this, and you're taking the first giant steps toward realizing your gift—toward achieving your extraordinary life.

Discovery Exercises

1. Put at the top of a sheet of paper your two highest values, your two strongest passions, and your two greatest strengths. From this list make different combinations of one value, one passion, and one strength. (There should be eight such combinations.)

2. Define your problem area (career, relationship, life balance, and so on). For purposes of this exercise, we'll use career as your problem area, but the Michelangelo Method works equally well for other areas.

3. Brainstorm three to five different careers that would be aligned with each of the eight combinations from step 1. For example, if one combination were harmony (value), teaching (passion), and physical dexterity (strength), one of the aligned careers might be yoga teacher. Another might be teaching gymnastics.

4. Rank each of the careers according to how well it is likely to satisfy all three criteria. The top five careers are good candidates for your career choice.

5. Contact people who are very successful in those careers. Interview them to find out what it takes to be successful in those fields and to determine what their life outside of work is like. Consider the feedback you receive in assessing your career choices. Pursue those career choices that continue to meet your needs.

The Battle of the Centaurs
The Battle of the Centaurs was carved for Lorenzo de'
Medici when Michelangelo was just seventeen years old.
Michelangelo used a claw-chisel coming at the marble from
different directions, re-creating the crisscross approach he
had practiced in drafting with pen and ink.
Photograph by Ken Schuman

3

....

Build on Your Strengths

So the boy continued drawing now one thing and now another, still without any settled workplace, or studio, when one day Granacci happened to take him to the garden of the Medici at San Marco, which Lorenzo the Magnificent, father of Pope Leo, a man distinguished for every kind of excellence, had adorned with various antique statues and figures. When Michelangelo had seen these, and tasted the beauty of the works to be found there, no longer did he go either to Domenico's workshop, or anywhere else, but instead all day long, as in the best school of all for this branch of art, stayed in the garden where he was always working.

—Life of Michelangelo,
Ascanio Condivi, 1553

Certainly, many of us enjoy sketching a silly face on a napkin to entertain our children at dinner. Or perhaps we simply enjoy doodling while chatting on the telephone. Some of us might even see making art as a passion. Perhaps we've taken a class in watercolor. Or maybe we spend the weekends upstate, sitting by our personal Walden Pond, easel placed on the rocky ground, dotting paints onto a canvas like some Sunday-afternoon Seurat. Maybe the life of a painter perfectly aligns our passions with our values. Maybe we wake in the middle of the night, our hearts full of dreams of being a painter.

I would like to say that such a person will no doubt become a master painter. But let's face it: some people, no matter how hard they train, will never be great. Even if you dream of being a painter, and even if the painter's life fits perfectly with the person you are deep down inside, without having an actual talent for painting, you will never—never, ever—create a masterpiece as a painter. To be a painter, you simply have to be able to paint.

In order to realize masterpieces in each of three fields, Michelangelo had to have a vision. He had to be able to see the masterpiece in the stone, in the form on the blank canvas, and in the building rising from the bare ground.

But vision is only part of an artist's success. To be an artist, one needs to have a talent for making art. Quite simply, an artist without an obedient hand cannot translate vision into art.

In order to truly master his media, Michelangelo needed one thing: the ability in his hands to render exactly what his eyes saw. He needed an obedient hand. For Michelangelo, the obedient hand was developed through his study of drawing. In developing the skill and dexterity to master the minute details of the human form in a pencil's line, Michelangelo learned to translate his vision into the gesture of the obedient hand.

Born to Draw

As a young boy, Michelangelo sketched avidly. Serving as an apprentice to the famed artist Ghirlandaio, Michelangelo spent day and night slaving over paper and charcoal. Whether he was drawing the human form, of both men and women, or secretly copying—and often improving upon—the sketches of his master in the middle of the night, Michelangelo devoted himself to his eye's perfection and the sharpening of his ability to master even the most minute forms in the subtle gestures of a hand or the sinews of a neck.

Even as the youngest apprentice in Ghirlandaio's studio, Michelangelo had strengths as a draftsman that rose above the crowd. In competition after competition, Michelangelo's skills trumped those of his peers, some of whom had been working with the master for years. And upon graduating from his apprentice-ship, Michelangelo had one of the most refined, obedient hands in all of Florence.

But what made Michelangelo's draftsmanship so integral to mastering multiple media was his ability to leverage this strength in all of his work to attain his vision. In sculpting, Michelangelo used his strengths in drawing to create elaborate sketches for the figures he saw inside the immense slabs of marble. In painting, his ability to focus on detail enabled him to create works of immense complexity and bring to life in a flurry of paint and brush what his mind could only imagine. In architecture, the lessons of form, structure, and proportion that he gained through patient study and drafting of anatomy enabled him to deeply understand the integral mathematical structures of building and to draft, with perfection, the blueprints for his architecture. In all of these media, Michelangelo leveraged his strengths.

Jack

Generally, when I first meet clients, the meetings tend to be at my home office. Occasionally, I make house calls and agree to meet my clients at their homes, at their workplaces, or, sometimes, even over the telephone when meeting face-to-face is an impossibility because of time or distance. Jack, however, was an exception. When I first met Jack, it was in the woods—in a dense forest that stretched over hundreds of preserved acres just miles from the heavily populated areas of suburban New Jersey.

Jack had given me precise directions for finding him in the woods. Before our meeting he had e-mailed me an image of a hand-drawn map of the trail that leads from a parking area on the woods' edge to a small clearing nearly a mile away. Loving a challenge and also a good autumn hike, I looked forward to meeting Jack in these idyllic surroundings.

Canopied by autumn leaves, I traipsed over the forest's rolling hills. I marveled at the natural beauty that I found here, so close to the trimmed lawns and highways. And at the end of this pleasant walk, I found Jack sitting high above the ground on a two-ton boulder.

He looked down at me from his perch like some suburban Puck—that mischievous imp of English folklore. His brown hiking boots dangled playfully over the rock's edge. A smile spread broadly upon his face. "Welcome to Silver Forest," he said.

⇒⇒ *Defend your turf.* ⇐⇐

As Jack and I sat there in the autumn sun, it was hard for me to believe that three years earlier Silver Forest had almost become the Silver Forest Development, a building site for a mammoth luxury condominium project. Back then, a group of local real estate developers had wanted to replace the native Douglas firs and oaks with winding roads and tightly packed housing units. Certainly, one could understand why; Silver Forest was an untapped plot, acres and acres of real estate in a community where properly zoned land could fetch hundreds of thousands of dollars per acre. With this condominium development, the investors could easily reap millions upon millions of dollars.

Still, while I could understand why local developers might want to develop Silver Forest, it was even easier to see why people—like Jack—might oppose the loss of this sylvan oasis.

Back when the words *Silver Forest* were first typed on real estate contracts, Jack had been working with a local chapter of a national environmental group. At one of their meetings, a group member, who at the time lived just off the edge of the forest, mentioned that surveyors were planting posts in the land just outside Silver Forest.

Jack tensed with suspicion and fear. He knew what was going on. It was the same thing that had gone on in this area since he was a child. Jack's hand shot up, and he took the floor to make a motion. Their group should investigate and determine what exactly was going on in Silver Forest.

*You don't measure progress
by the number of strip malls.*

Jack had been concerned with environmental preservation ever since he was a young boy. He had grown up around these woods of suburban New Jersey and as Jack marked his height on the bedroom door frame, the size of the neighboring towns grew as well. Towns that once had barely a thousand residents quickly expanded to tens of thousands. Strip malls began to dot the landscape to service these new residents who were looking to live in an atmosphere where nature and convenience met.

During this time, Jack's family was involved in the community. His parents would sit in town council meetings, talking about the risks expansion created for natural diversity, and many a dinner table conversation about the issues continued through the evening, keeping him in constant awareness of the challenges their community faced.

However, Jack wasn't poring over legal papers in the local library; rather, Jack was out playing in the very woods that would later become his passion.

After school, Jack and his brothers would all head into the small forest near their home. There, they would build forts in rocky crevices and play capture the flag until dinnertime. Then, mud staining the knees of their jeans, they would head back to the family dinner table and recount tales of their adventures.

With summer's warm nights and freedom from school, Jack and his brothers sometimes wouldn't trek home at all. Sleeping bags tied to their backpacks, they would hike still deeper into the woods and camp out under the stars. Lying on the ground, Jack would mark the constellations, his eyes filling with wonder at the immensity of the natural world.

Despite all the changes he had seen, Jack had never lost that sense of wonder and play, nor had he ever lost the passion he felt for the forest of his childhood. But the path of Jack's life did not lead him directly to working with this lifelong passion, the environment.

>>> *Align your career with your values and passions.* <<<

Looking at Jack here in Silver Forest bounding down from the boulder, I found it hard to believe I was looking at the director of marketing for one of the "Big Five" accounting firms. Of course, this dissonance just might have been why Jack and I were meeting. Jack had realized that his career was completely out of alignment with his values and passions.

The lay of Jack's career track was carved with perseverance and followed the ascent of success. Jack had graduated from a prestigious liberal arts school with a double major in English and philosophy. While he had excelled in school, his degree left him, as his mother would say, "doubly unemployable." Not one to be set back by the traditional workings of the world, Jack blazed his own path of employment.

⟫ *Initiative is often rewarded.* ⟪

Recognizing his strength in communications, Jack found work first as a technical writer at a technology company. Innately entrepreneurial and also lucky to find himself in a small department that encouraged such out-of-the-box thinking, Jack soon created opportunities to employ his skills. When he recognized his company didn't have a corporate newsletter, he decided to go ahead and start one himself. Soon he was creating a whole series of communications to the community of workers. The next thing Jack knew, he had established a position for himself as the manager of corporate communications.

Recognizing a career when he saw it and wanting to ensure his family's financial security over the long haul, Jack began to plot a career track for himself. An opportunity arose for Jack to be manager of public affairs at an aerospace firm. Understanding that he would need more management and public relations experience to achieve his ultimate goal of being a director of communications and vice president of a large company, Jack snapped it up.

Things got even better when his company landed the contract for the space shuttle. Working with the launch of the shuttle, Jack was able to marry his job to his fascination with the natural world. Working as the PR liaison for all the space shuttle's test flights, Jack traveled the world promoting the news of the shuttle's progress. He even got to travel to Washington to lobby for the shuttle program in the U.S. Senate. All the while, Jack honed the communications skills that would help him in the future.

Working closely with the vice president for communications, he received important lessons in motivating teams to bring projects in on time and tracking multiple projects within the Byzantine systems of a complex multinational organization. In addition, by being forced to deal with external communications, Jack learned an entirely new area related to his field.

>>> *We all need to refresh ourselves; otherwise we burn out.* <<<

But even though this exciting job exercised his strengths, it wasn't enough to keep Jack energized. In the high-stress and competitive atmosphere, Jack found himself burning out. And while Jack managed to refresh himself by remaining active in various environmental issues outside of his job, without that work being central to his life, he felt something was missing. For ultimately, it wasn't just the wonder of nature that was Jack's passion, it was his ability to help make a difference in preserving the natural world that was an integral value.

Jack discovered what was really going on in Silver Forest during a long afternoon at the local library. There he uncovered a series of public records that revealed an agreement to develop Silver Forest. His worst fears were realized.

Needing to investigate further, he and his group attended the monthly meeting of their town council. After the council went through the usual discussions of school budgets and Memorial Day parade routes, they opened the floor to the community. Jack, versed in lobbying from his work on the space shuttle, was chosen by the group to ask the question, what was happening to Silver Forest?

Jack stepped up to the podium and fired off a volley of sharp questions. When the members of the council attempted to circumvent his questions with cryptic responses, Jack produced a copy of the public records from his jacket. He inquired about the deal described in the records. "Why hadn't this been brought before the people of the town?"

The council balked, caught off guard by Jack's expert presentation. Jack's heart grew loud in his chest.

Jack pressed his case. "Why hasn't this been placed for a public vote?" he demanded.

The council responded again, this time with even vaguer platitudes and a warning that he was "out of order." Jack was not to be deterred. He again pressed his case. This time, the council asked him to step down.

Then it happened. One by one, the members of Jack's group lined up behind the microphone. One member of the group stepped up and asked the same questions that Jack had asked. When the council silenced that member, the next person in line continued the process, until each member had been silenced and the meeting was adjourned.

But that was only one meeting. Everyone who was there that night knew that Jack and his group were not finished. A movement had been born.

>>> *Build on your strengths to achieve your most important goals.* <<<

By this time, Jack had left his job managing communications at the aerospace firm and had taken an even more challenging position as corporate communications manager at a leading public accounting firm. Jack had reached the next rung on the ladder of success toward his ultimate career goal.

Even with his new responsibilities, Jack spent every free moment working to save Silver Forest, all the while using the communications strengths he had developed in his professional career. Jack drafted press releases and persuaded local reporters to write stories on the history of the forest, the forest's importance to the state's ecosystem, and the development that would erase it from the town. A letter-writing campaign was initiated. The group went door-to-door with petitions of protest. They attended monthly meetings of the town council to voice their dissent.

Their ranks grew. Soon the entire audience of town council meetings was filled with people protesting the destruction of Silver Forest. The council members began to look pale at the start of each meeting.

It was August when turnout reached its peak. All that month, Jack and his group had been organizing a campaign to get an initiative about Silver Forest's development on the November ballot. This would be their last chance to persuade the council to bring the referendum to the people.

When the matter of the vote came up, more than a hundred people lined up at the microphone to voice their concern—all of them in favor of saving Silver Forest. One by one they spoke about the importance of Silver Forest in their lives: how their children played in the woods, how they would jog the trails every morning, how they had proposed to their wife in the shade of the pine trees.

Jack stood at the end of the line to make the final plea for a ballot referendum. He spoke with great passion, his wife and son at his side. "We are the people of this town. And we, the people, deserve to be heard before such an integral part of our town's landscape is to be altered forever. That is why we come to you today and ask that you give the people a chance to cast their vote this November on the development of Silver Forest."

Applause broke out in the back of the room and filtered forward like a wave. Gavels were struck to stem the tide and bring the room back to order. Finally, the vote was held, one by one the council members saying yea or nay on the ballot initiative. The vote was tied. The powerful mayor was to cast the last vote, the vote that would break the deadlock and determine the fate of Silver Forest. Silence fell over the room until the vote was cast. The vote was yea.

⇛ *Follow up on your successes with increased energy.* ⇚

Jack's campaign had worked. The ballot initiative was on. By using his strength in marketing and communications in serving his values and passions, Jack was able to rally the town in support of Silver Forest. Now, with the referendum pending, there was no time to rest. Jack's work to save Silver Forest shifted into high gear.

For the next few months, Jack's motivation for his corporate work paled in comparison to his passion for preserving the environment. Jack had achieved yet another rung on the success ladder: director of marketing for the chemicals and pharmaceuticals sector. His professional goals of wealth and recognition were becoming a reality, but he began to feel that there was more to his life than a fat paycheck and an occasional "atta boy" from his boss.

Unlike his previous company, where Jack's entrepreneurial spirit was valued and rewarded, here at the public accounting firm, the team-spirit slogans pinned on the company bulletin boards spoke false testimony to the actual goings-on at the office. In reality, every department was an isolated fiefdom ruled by possessive masters—the firm's partners. And these fiefdoms were eternally in conflict, each day fighting vigorously over territory and resources.

Meanwhile, Jack's insistence on taking on the cause of Silver Forest had made him none too popular with his superiors at work. He had been warned to ease off his extracurricular activities as the firm provided accounting services to one of the major developer groups.

As Jack's relationships at work began to deteriorate, the effort needed to continue going into the office grew greater. When he would wake in the morning, thoughts of escape bounced like pinballs in his head. Sometimes he'd stand in the shower, water running over him for minutes at a time, wishing that he could stand there and the day would be washed away into the next day.

When November rolled around—and with it the decision on the fate of Silver Forest—Jack didn't need to know the outcome to know his own fate. It wasn't just Silver Forest that needed saving; it was Jack himself.

With whispers of coming layoffs percolating through the office cafeteria, Jack discovered his escape route. Knowing that he was becoming a source of friction, Jack recognized that his leaving the company would be a welcome event. Walking into his boss's office, Jack made a bold proposition: "Give me a package, and I'll leave quietly." The next thing Jack knew, he was presented with a release package that would give him the time and financial security to find more fulfilling work.

Jack jogged out the door with a shopping bag of personal items— the last artifacts of a past life—then hopped into his car and drove. When he came to his home, something pushed him to just keeping driving.

He soon found himself a few miles north at his childhood home. Parking his car along the side of the road, Jack took the path off the side into the woods where he used to play as a child.

As the sun set, he walked past the stream where he raced frogs with his brother, past the rock that served as base for capture the flag. He sat on a log and let silence fall over him. He looked up at the dusk and wondered if it would rain the next day.

After weeks of work, Jack and his wife cast their votes against the development of Silver Forest. Early the following morning, all the members of the environmental group decided to meet at a local coffee shop to wait for the delivery of the morning's news. When the delivery truck pulled up and the driver saw them all there huddled over tables, the newspaper deliveryman couldn't help but break out into a smile. As he laid the bale of newspapers on the ground, Jack rushed to pull a paper from the top of the stack. There, on the front page of the local news section, a headline stood out, bold as the morning's coffee: "COMMUNITY STOPS SILVER FOREST DEVELOPMENT."

⇒⇒ *Call upon your strengths when changing direction.* ⇐⇐

When Jack told me his story, I learned a lot about the man sitting before me in the beauty of the forest he had helped to save. This was a man who knew what he valued in his life. This was a man who was passionate about something. And yet, I also knew that this was a man who was still unsure of how he could transform his vision into a viable career—the career he knew he had always wanted.

Jack knew he had wanted to help preserve nature. What he didn't know was how to make a living preserving nature. "I've spent my whole career working toward this one goal, to become the head of a corporate communications department. And now that I've realized it's not my calling, I'm at a loss. I just want to start over."

"Why would you want to start over?" I asked.

The answer to Jack seemed obvious. "Well, so I could start doing something important. I could have studied environmental science in college, or I could have gotten into politics. There were a hundred

things I could have done." With that Jack trailed off, his mind lost
to the tangle of the woods.

"How did you save this forest, Jack?"

Jack's eyes returned to mine. An idea was forming. The fact was
he had saved this forest not because he had started over doing something he had always wanted to do but because he had worked with
the strengths he had developed over time. Without the skills in
communications—strengths in writing, speaking, and public relations honed over years working for top corporations—Jack would
never have been able to rally such an overwhelming charge to end
the Silver Forest development. Like Michelangelo, he was able to
succeed because he had the strengths and skills to translate his
vision into reality.

Now, if Jack were going to make the same breakthrough in his
career, he would need to build upon these very strengths to realize his vision for preserving the environment. Jack didn't need to
start over. He needed to start thinking how he could continue to
work with and expand his strengths as he followed his vision. If Jack
could do that, he wouldn't just find a position where he could save
the environment; he would find a position where he could also save
himself. We'll follow Jack through this passage in later chapters.

Michelangelo in Crisis

You're in a crisis. Your world is falling apart. You feel weak, confused, panicky. Here's some good advice: when in crisis, harness
your strengths. They will lead you to your comfort zone; you'll
begin to be able to think clearly and find your way.

Michelangelo was frequently in crisis. Popes Julius II, Leo X,
Clement VII, and Paul III were extremely demanding bosses. And
because they were constantly beset by wars and short of money, they

paid little and paid slowly, often putting Michelangelo in financial crisis.

How did Michelangelo deal with these crises? He went straight to his strengths—his absolute commitment to his work, his extraordinary drafting ability, and his unshakable faith in a responsive God.

Pressure from the Boss

In 1507 Pope Julius II, "the warrior Pope," led the Vatican army in its successful conquest of Bologna. To celebrate this victory, Julius ordered Michelangelo to cast a huge equestrian statue of the pope in bronze, which would be placed in front of San Petronio Basilica, which was still under construction and was intended to be the largest Catholic church in the world. Julius made it clear that this project was extremely important to him. That put lots of pressure on Michelangelo to get it done quickly and to get it done right. But bronze was not Michelangelo's medium, and he lacked experience in casting in metal.

Here's a modern-day equivalent. Your boss insists that you must do her pet project, which she sees as her permanent legacy to the future. The project is extraordinarily complicated. Worse yet, you lack the relevant experience necessary to succeed. Big-time crisis. How do you avoid paralysis? If research is your strength, you would be well advised to recognize this, calm yourself, and hit the books. This familiar process will help you get calm and focused for the next steps.

➤➤ *When in crisis, turn to your strengths.* ◀◀

Michelangelo's response to crisis was to throw himself into the design of the work and pray for God's guidance. He summarized the result in a letter written November 30, 1507, to his brother Buonarroto: "I have endured and am enduring such labor that if I had another such again I don't think my life would be long enough. ... But I think that the prayers of a few people have helped me and kept me healthy, for it was contrary to the opinion of all Bologna that I would ever get it completed after it was cast; and even earlier no one believed that I would ever cast it."

Michelangelo's most serious crises were related to his health. Living in unsanitary conditions in the midst of war, famine, and plague, he from time to time became dangerously ill. In 1531 Giovan Battista Mini, after visiting the "shriveling" Michelangelo, wrote to the pope's commissioner, Bartolommeo Valori, that Michelangelo "has been made invalid by catarrh, headaches, and dizziness" and predicted that he would soon die. Michelangelo responded again by moving to his strengths, praying that God protect his health and redoubling efforts to finish statues he had been working on for the Medici family. When Michelangelo was at work, his juices flowed. He found his work healing. Michelangelo, then fifty-six, lived another thirty-three years.

Maggie

Maggie had just turned fifty years old. She had a good job in market research and a successful marriage with two great kids. Her twenty-two-year-old son, Josh, was about to graduate from college, and her twenty-five-year-old daughter, Lisa, was engaged to be married. Maggie was helping to plan the wedding.

Now some people would have just thanked their lucky stars, knocked on wood, or, in Maggie's Jewish faith, kept the evil eye away by saying "pooh-pooh." But Maggie's eyes were on bigger things. Fifty meant middle age, and Maggie had the ambition to start her own marketing company. She was nervous, though, about the risks involved. She was in many ways a conservative person who liked to play things safe. On the other hand, if she was going to start her own business, she believed that she should start now. She came to me for help.

We were beginning to go over the potential risks and rewards of entrepreneurial life when Maggie's world fell apart. We kept going with our sessions, making some progress here and there. But much of the time I just tried to support her in her efforts to get through the day.

Her son, Josh, had just been diagnosed with lymphoma, a potentially fatal cancer, in his chest.

"I'm so scared, I'm nearly paralyzed," she told me.

⟫⟫ *Generally, the more you know, the less you have to fear.* ⟪⟪

"Perhaps educating yourself about Josh's problem would ease your mind," I suggested. "You can use the research skills that serve you so well at work to find out what you can do for Josh."

Maggie brightened a little. "That's a thought," she said. "Usually, the more I know about something, the more comfortable I am. It's when I know little or nothing that I get crazy."

Maggie went online to learn what she could. She found out that while lymphoma can be fatal, many people fully recover. Assuming that Josh's diagnosis was correct, his chances were better than fifty-fifty.

Maggie and her husband, Steve, needed to get a second opinion. Another research project for Maggie. She discovered that her sister's former husband was engaged to a pediatric oncologist. "They parted on good terms, and he still comes to family functions with their kids," Maggie explained. "His fiancée was a huge source of help. She referred me to a close friend of hers, a specialist in lymphoma at Mt. Sinai Hospital, which I knew from my research has one of the best oncology departments in the country. He did us a huge favor and saw Josh in two days. After some extensive procedures, he confirmed the diagnosis. He was very kind and considerate and answered all our questions. We decided to use him as Josh's primary physician."

But the reality of Josh's illness and the possibility that he might not survive were sinking in. "That was one of the worst nights of my entire life," Maggie said. "I was in bed shaking the whole night. I just couldn't make my mind think constructive thoughts. Fear just took over." We discussed what strengths Maggie could use to cope with her crisis. In addition to research, Maggie's strengths included her networking ability, resilience, sense of humor, and faith in God. She could rely on these to help her deal with this crisis.

But first she had to calm herself. I asked her if she wanted me to make a visualization tape for her. "I'd be really grateful for anything that can ease my mind," she said. Later she told me that this tape was one of the best tools she had for coping with Josh's problem.

On the tape I asked Maggie to think about Josh in the future. To think about him speaking to groups of people and telling them how he licked his problem and became a better person for it. To picture herself dancing with Josh at his wedding five years from now. And to picture herself in the doctor's office and the doctor saying to Josh, "You're cured!" Also, to picture Josh, encased in a bubble, with sun shining on him, sending him healing energy. And to picture Josh floating with her on a lake, being calm and being healed.

Maggie also tried to find support within her community. "My husband and I have a very good relationship, but it became too painful to talk to him about some of this. It was easier to talk to people who were less connected," she said. "After Josh got sick I couldn't sleep," Maggie continued. "I would wake up very early in the morning. So I went to the early morning service at my temple. The people were very warm and welcoming. In the beginning I would just sit there and cry. One man had been through cancer and survived. One had a son who had had cancer in high school and recovered. So I talked to them; that helped.

"I'm very fatalistic," Maggie added. "I wasn't angry. I never said, 'Why me? Why Josh?' In fact, when one of my friends said, 'Oh, it shouldn't have been Josh,' I responded, 'Oh, then it should have been someone else's child?' It is what it is. I did have the belief that God had the power to cure him and heal him if that was the plan."

Maggie believed in the power of prayer. "I told everyone I knew about it and asked everyone, no matter what their religion, to pray for him. I obviously prayed for his healing," she said. "But part of what I would pray for was for all of us to be strong so that we could get through this."

⟫ *Don't underestimate the power of your beliefs.* ⟪

Josh was diagnosed in July, and fortunately things were slowing down for the summer at Maggie's company. Her boss was very understanding and agreed to give Maggie two months' leave to be with Josh and care for him. Josh started chemotherapy treatments. He mostly responded well but had a bad reaction to the prednisone he was taking and started hallucinating. "That was very scary for Josh—he thought he was going crazy," Maggie said. "We needed to go to a psychopharmacologist, who reduced his dosage."

Maggie researched support groups for him. Josh went to one. "It was awful," Maggie reported. "There were lots of people in terminal situations, and it was dreadful for him to hear their stuff." But she did find a program that matched him up with someone in his age group who had a similar diagnosis and who had successfully been through his experience. That turned out to be a big help.

"I'm a bit 'woo-woo,' if you know what I mean, and wanted to take Josh to a hypnotherapist and an herbalist, thinking maybe that might help him. But he didn't want any of that. A friend gave me this one piece of very good advice: 'He's twenty-two years old. He's not a baby. The more you can treat him like an adult, the better. Let him run his own case whenever you can.' So I tried to do that—to take a step back, be respectful of him, and let him make choices."

⇒⇒ *Learn how to set limits.* ⇐⇐

One day Maggie plopped down on the chair in my office and said, "My friends are making me crazy. They call up and ask a million questions. I don't know what they think gives them the right to do that. They ask, 'What is his diagnosis anyway?' Everyone means well, but it's just overwhelming. It's too painful. My cousin who does cancer research in Washington said to me, 'If you can get past the first eighteen months, you're past the period of potential relapses.' Do I have to hear this garbage?"

That meeting we worked on setting boundaries. "You've got to avoid people and situations that erode your strength," I advised. We decided that Maggie would give her best friend, Joan, regular updates about Josh's progress, and everyone else would be referred to her. Maggie would tell people that it was too draining for her to answer the questions individually.

A Time to Dance

Lisa's wedding was coming up. "Josh wanted to give them money as a gift, but I urged him to give them a real present because in case, God forbid, something should happen to him, I wanted them to have received something concrete from him for the wedding. I didn't tell Josh my reason, of course."

Josh had been making excellent progress with his treatments, so Lisa's wedding that November was a truly joyous affair. Josh provided a very funny "brother's toast" to the newlyweds.

The session after the wedding Maggie was very upbeat but was concerned that Josh had been out of the loop with his friends, all of whom were starting new jobs or going into graduate school programs. I told her that Josh may be behind his friends now, but when he finished his treatment he'd be light-years ahead of them because of all that he would have learned about himself and life. Maggie told me that was a very helpful comment, and it stayed with her. "I keep trying to focus on that," she said.

With Josh's illness and Lisa's wedding, Maggie's family had been a center of people's attention. After the wedding Josh had commented, "At least now we're out of the spotlight." Then two weeks later came the accident.

A Time to Mourn

Maggie's mother and father, who lived in Florida, were driving home late one night. Their car crossed the divider and was hit by a large truck. Her father had perhaps fallen asleep at the wheel, or he may have had a heart attack. Maggie would never know for sure—both of her parents were killed instantly. "When my parents died I was numb. I felt like I was going out of my mind. I was falling apart. I went to my rabbi once or twice. He recommended a therapist to go to. I went there once, but I didn't think he was helpful.

"I thought a lot about their deaths, and the fatalistic part of me felt that in a way they died so that Josh could live, as weird as that might sound. Because now they are up there and maybe they can help. But I also felt very guilty. When Josh got sick, Steve and I were the only people in our age group to have all four parents still living. We have a long tradition of dark humor in my family—my grandfather was a stand-up comedian who played the Catskills. Steve and I joked that we would be willing to trade a parent for Josh. A part of me thinks I killed them.

"Steve, Josh, Lisa, and I all gave eulogies at my parents' funeral. When Josh had spoken at the wedding, he was bald with no eyebrows and no eyelashes. He got up at the funeral and spoke about his grandparents, and then he said, 'This is the last time I make a public speech bald. The next time I make a speech, I want to have hair.' "

Three weeks later Josh developed a cough, which was one of the original symptoms of his cancer. "I was taking him to his doctor's appointment and was feeling that I was cracking up," Maggie said. "I was just so scared. I was thinking that, God forbid, Josh was relapsing. And I was feeling that I couldn't go through that again. After I dropped Josh off, I was walking down the hall and saw a sign for Cancer Care. I went in and asked if there were any support groups for mothers of young adults who have cancer and who also had both parents recently killed in a car accident. The woman was soooo sweet. She said, 'Oh my God. We have a person who's here today, and she might be able to see you.' She told me to come back later, and she would try to squeeze me in, which she did. I had a wonderful session with her. She is a social worker and counseled me for free. I must have gone to her six times. She was absolutely wonderful."

The cough went away—it turned out to be a minor cold. Josh continued progressing with his treatments. "He recovered completely, thank God," Maggie said. "He's thirty-one, married, with a baby of his own. Now Josh helps others. Anytime anyone who has cancer wants to talk to him, Josh will make the time. Also, if there's a mother who needs to talk, I'll make myself available, because I know what I went through."

⇢ *Find strength in adversity.* ⇠

Through her experience with Josh, Maggie developed a different attitude toward risk, which spilled over into all other areas of her life. For she had confronted her worst fear, the potential death of a child, and, using her existing strengths, had come through it intact. Better than intact. For her faith in her ability to deal with her worst nightmares was strengthened as was her faith in the future. So when we returned to work on whether Maggie should start her own marketing company, I found we were no longer discussing "whether" but rather "how" to make her concept a reality.

Over our next few meetings, we created a business plan, after which Maggie gave notice and set up shop. Her first clients came quickly as a number of companies with whom she had worked chose to hire her, a harbinger of other successes that were to follow.

The Greeting Cards Arrive

At our last session, Maggie brought in a big box filled with greeting cards. "People in our community like to send cards," Maggie said. "When Josh got sick, people felt funny sending us a card until they sensed how things were going to end up. So after the funeral when it looked like, God willing, he was going to be OK, we got cards for everything that had gone on: 'Congratulations on your daughter's wedding, may Josh be well and live a long and wonderful life, and sorry about your parents' deaths.' So I had to write them a note back: 'Thanks for your good wishes about the wedding, thanks for your kind regards for Josh's recovery, and thank you for your caring note regarding my parents' deaths.'

"I can talk about all this now, because the passing of time has been healing with regard to my parents and both of my kids are doing great." She added, "Knock on wood; pooh-pooh."

Sculpt Your Personal Masterpiece

Artists have more than a vision. They also have the talent and ability to bring their vision to life. They have the obedient hand that can translate their mind's creation into something tangible.

No doubt, vision is integral to breaking through to an extraordinary career, but it's just as integral to develop your strengths to achieve that vision. First, you need to look objectively at the knowledge and skills you've nurtured and see how they fit with your personal values and passions. Then you must evaluate your talents and undertake the hard work to develop them further.

Without his strength in drawing, Michelangelo could never have succeeded as an artist, no matter how much confidence or determination he had. Without developing his talents in marketing and communications, Jack would not have been able to save Silver Forest. Maggie's research skills and social intelligence helped her deal with her son's potentially fatal illness.

Ask yourself these questions:

+ What are my strengths?

+ What strengths do I need to build to achieve success in all areas of my life: career, financial, relationships, environment, spiritual, and other areas that are important to me?

+ How can I best build these strengths?

+ What would be the benefit to me and to others when I build those strengths?

Discovery Exercises

1. Examine the strengths that you just identified. Consider how each relates to achieving your goals. If your goal is to enter a new field or build a business, conduct research to identify the skills

and qualifications needed. A good start is to use the Internet to narrow down your choices. For example, entering the search term "careers in photography" yielded 29,200 hits using a popular search engine. It usually is helpful to put the search terms in quotation marks to narrow your search (without the quotation marks, more than 34 million results were returned). Peruse the top-listed sites first and you'll probably have more than enough information to get started. We have listed a few sites that provide information about many careers, including qualifications required to enter the field. See Appendix B for links to those sites as well as recommended books to assist you in selecting a career choice that fits you.

2. Another tool to assist you in making a career choice is career assessment testing. We use assessment testing in our coaching practice and find that it helps our clients to quickly understand their competencies and strengths. Coaches, career counselors, and career-services organizations can provide professional assessment testing. Be sure that the coach or counselor is certified in the assessment instruments being used. Many career assessment tests are available online for free or for a minimal charge. We don't recommend these because there us usually no feedback provided by a trained and certified professional to interpret the results and relate the insights provided to your specific situation.

3. Set up informational interviews with three to five people who are already in this field and have achieved success. Most people enjoy speaking about their work and will readily give you twenty to thirty minutes of their time. Find them through referrals from the people in your network, reading articles, or career coaches. Ask what attracted them to this career, profession, or business. Determine what education, background, training, skills, and

credentials are needed. Find out what the most important factors for their success were and what roadblocks they encountered along their journey. Ask what advice they would give to someone contemplating or starting to prepare for a career in their field. Ask what values and behaviors were important to their success. (Your way of being is just as important as your credentials in achieving your masterpiece.) Finally, ask if they could refer you to a colleague or another source of information. Now that you understand what you need to be successful, make a list of all the skills, work and life experience, hobbies, education, and training you have that relates to success in your chosen career.

4. Compare your current qualifications to the qualifications you need to be successful, and identify any gaps in education, experience, training, credentials, and so on. The difference is the gap you need to close in order to enter and achieve success in your new field or business. Create a plan to close the gap through additional training, licensing, education, credentials, work experience, and skills development.

5. If your goals are life goals or, as in Maggie's case, life's emergencies, take an inventory of your strengths and determine what's missing that you need in order to be successful in achieving your vision. Consider not only what you need to be able to do but also what kind of person you need to be in order to achieve success and mastery. Consider your own emotional intelligence and where improvements might be needed to manage your current situation. Close gaps in your life skills such as self-awareness, self-management, conflict management, and empathetic outlook by working with professionals such as therapists, counselors, and coaches, depending on your needs. Many coaches offer assessments to help you understand your own behavioral styles

and emotional intelligence. Also consider education and training programs that can support you in developing life skills, such as those offered by the Omega Institute (eomega.org) and The Learning Annex (learningannex.com).

6. Review your plan with your coach or other people you trust, and seek feedback and suggestions for improvement.

Now you are ready to execute your plan and refine it as needed.

Bacchus
Michelangelo produced the *Bacchus* when he was twenty-two years old, after being challenged by Cardinal Riario, a patron, to produce a beautiful, original life-size statue rather than continuing to copy antiquities.
Photograph by Ron Paxton

4
. . . .
Commit to Your Vision with Confidence

All the time that Michelangelo could snatch, he would spend in drawing in secret, being scolded for this by his father and his other elders, and at times beaten. They perchance considered that to give attention to that art, which was not known by them, was a mean thing and not worthy of their ancient house. As the desire to work at art grew greater everyday in Michelangelo, his father perceived that he could not divert the boy from giving his attention to design, and that there was no help for it.

—Life of Michelangelo,
Giorgio Vasari, 1568

Masterpieces are born in adversity. Sculptures start in stone and sometimes, like Michelangelo's *David*, in damaged stone. Some great works encounter their obstacle halfway, in an errant brushstroke, bad planning, illness, people intent on sabotaging good work or being critical each step of the way, or sometimes our own criticism, in our own destructive belief that a masterpiece is not to come from these "weak" hands.

To create your masterpiece, to break through the obstacles that hold back your career and your life, requires a commitment to a process, a process of creating and failing and creating again.

But perhaps more important than the quality of your commitment is your confidence in the commitment. To achieve your masterpiece you need to focus on your vision no matter what stands in its way. You must harness the inner strength to master inevitable failures and to leap over the immovable obstacles. Most important, you must have an overriding knowledge that you *can* accomplish all these things.

⇒⟩ *Great works require faith.* ⟨⇐

In short, great works require faith. Not necessarily a religious faith, but a faith in the integrity of your vision and in the vast potential of your abilities. Without this, achieving mastery is impossible. But hold this faith, and mastery isn't merely possible, but it comes with grace.

Even as a young child, Michelangelo was committed to his vision of being an artist. But Michelangelo's father, Ludovico, had another vision for his son. Lodovico wanted his son to be the most successful businessman in Florence.

Ludovico Buonarroti would accept nothing less from his son. After all, though Lodovico had only a tenuous connection to the ruling Medici family, the Buonarroti name had a pedigree, a place in Florentine society. They were not a family of artists! Artists were poor creatures who huddled in dank studios, whose lot was obscurity and poverty. The Buonarrotis were an ancient house of businessmen. They made money, not masterpieces!

Unfortunately, when Michelangelo was a boy, the Buonarroti family wasn't making much money at all. And Lodovico watched his status dwindle with his family's fortunes. So when Michelangelo showed the glint of intelligence and promise, Lodovico pinned his family's hopes upon him. Lodovico sent him to be schooled in grammar and mathematics.

Lodovico dreamed that Michelangelo had a place at the bountiful table of elite society, an honored guest of the Medici—a true figure of wealth in Florentine society. One day, Michelangelo would become the successful businessman that Lodovico never was.

(Don't be deterred from following your passions simply to please others.

Michelangelo, however, was not to be deterred from his own passions simply because of his father's wishes. As he studied grammar, Michelangelo stole time for his drawing, spending hour upon hour sketching figures, designs, and anatomies.

This raised Lodovico's ire. When Ludovico caught Michelangelo with a drawing pen in hand, he would remove the pen from the boy's fingers. He would tear up the sketches the boy had been working on. And then Lodovico would slap his son's face and even beat him, hoping that this discipline would shake him from these artistic dreams.

But Michelangelo suffered the beatings as a matter of course, as just another obstacle along the way. When his father had left him, he would dry his tears and return to his drawings, his commitment even greater and his faith in himself even stronger.

Ultimately, the strength of Michelangelo's resolve overcame his father's will. After Michelangelo's good friend Francesco Granacci began an apprenticeship as an artist, Michelangelo gathered the courage to join him. Secretly, he rushed off to the studio of master artist Domenico Ghirlandaio and convinced the brusque master to take him as his pupil.

When the boy—the fire of commitment in his eyes—told his father of his new course of study, Ludovico realized that nothing would deter Michelangelo from pursuing his vision. Reluctantly, he pulled his son from his academic studies and allowed him to begin his apprenticeship to Ghirlandaio.

⇢⇢ *The master is not always right.* ⇠⇠

In Ghirlandaio's studio, one of the primary methods of teaching was to have students copy the works of his own hands. When a student could render a good copy of the master's drawings, then he was allowed to draw from life. Only then could he begin to become a master in his own right.

One day the young apprentices were copying Ghirlandaio's sketches of women draped in cloth. The students fixed closely on the lines of the drawing, attempting to reproduce on their own paper the particular slope of the women's bodies, the curve of their fingers, the lineaments of the drapery upon their hips—all from the master's original line.

All except for Michelangelo. He not only saw his master's work, he saw through it.

Looking at one of the originals, Michelangelo realized that the drape of the cloth did not heed the anatomy of the woman's body underneath. Rather than copy a drawing that was not true to life, and confident in his understanding of that truth, Michelangelo put down his pen. He snatched the paper from which the other apprentices were copying, placed it before himself, and selected a wider pen. Michelangelo's hand moved confidently over the master's drawing, augmenting it, creating a thicker line that corrected the cloth's drape to take account of the body beneath it.

Michelangelo had not only the boldness to correct his master's work but the ability to do so. When he finished, the apprentices gathered around with envy and wonder.

In addition to having the strength to translate his vision into art, Michelangelo had a fire inside him—a fire that would drive him to overcome any obstacles and a confident commitment to his own vision. And while you might imagine this sort of impetuous behavior would have earned Michelangelo a punishment, the reality was quite the contrary. Michelangelo's confidence caught the eye of his master, Ghirlandaio.

When the ruler of Florence, Lorenzo de' Medici, established a school for sculpture, he sent his men out to the greatest artists of the day to discover the young artists who had the skill and conviction to master the form and become the world's greatest sculptors. When they reached Ghirlandaio, his choice was Michelangelo.

Ultimately, with his success as a sculptor, Michelangelo remained true to his vision and also garnered the recognition and status from the Medici family of which his father had always dreamed. For Michelangelo's faith in his vision and talent impressed all those he met. Patrons, artists, and others who watched the young Michelangelo work had no doubt that he would become the greatest artist of his generation. No matter what obstacles lay before him, nothing could stop Michelangelo. He was ready to take on the world.

Catherine

A year before I met her, it seemed nothing could stop Catherine. There she was, working with a hot software company whose market was growing exponentially. Investor financing rushed into the company like a river. New software businesses spun off, seemingly daily. And with her expertise in managing clients, experience gained from administering information technology networks in large corporations, Catherine was positioned to be a key player. Before you could say "dot-com," Catherine found herself, with the title of director of customer relations, responsible for overseeing customer relations for a new enterprise and getting a six-figure salary. Catherine was ready to take on the world.

But this was the 1990s. And in the 1990s, business was a game of chance and speculation.

First, as the '90s ramped up, the rapid pace of authentic innovation excited the market. With emerging technologies opening possibilities for new businesses, many smart young entrepreneurs were creating viable new businesses. But as the decade rolled to a close, innovation began to be replaced by hustle.

Surprisingly, these misguided hustlers did not deter venture capitalists. Nor did they deter the market. In fact, the race to the next big business grew flush with hysteria, and the bubble of speculation grew in the market. That bubble was sure to burst. And when it did, Catherine was sure to be right beneath it.

Catherine, as we will also see in a later chapter, was a woman of extraordinary ability. She wasn't just good at her job. Catherine was great. She had a can-do attitude. She had superior customer service skills. More than that, she had the insight to save her company a good deal of money on a monthly basis. Catherine had talent.

The company's president took notice. He began to spend more time with Catherine. Once a week they would sit down for lunch, and he would discuss with her the responsibilities of his job and what he had learned over the course of his tenure. At work he would consult her on difficult questions and sometimes show her how he solved particularly difficult issues.

You might say Catherine had become his apprentice. She quickly learned the issues and skills in the job of managing corporate operations. With her sharp mind, interest in learning, and diverse skill set, Catherine quickly absorbed the president's lessons, and when he talked of the company going public, he assured Catherine that a vice presidency and a hefty bonus, on top of the stock options she already earned, would make her wealthy.

One night Catherine drove to dinner, her mind racing with the possibility of achieving such a high position in her career. And the prospect of cashing out her stock options would give her the financial security she could only have dreamed about in the past. Catherine was going to be a dot-com millionaire.

She relayed the news to her boyfriend over appetizers. Her boyfriend signaled the waiter for a bottle of champagne.

Back then they called it the New Economy. Technology wasn't all that had changed. The way companies fueled their growth had changed as well. Where once companies grew organically, now they grew through mergers and public offerings. Like any time of great change, it was an exciting time to live. And a volatile one.

Catherine's company was ripe for some New Economy–style growth. And when the president of Catherine's company announced a merger with a foreign company that would provide funds to fuel the company's growth leading to a public stock offering, no one was surprised.

On the day of the announcement, Catherine sat in the conference room among all the other employees. There was buzz in the room. What was going to happen next? The president strode to the lectern. Catherine did a double take as he announced that the new vice president position, which Catherine had been promised, would go to a man less competent than she.

Such was the way of the New Economy. With the merger and their investment, the new foreign company of course expected a voice in running things. As Catherine would come to learn, this company had a male-dominated culture where women were considered inferior.

A week later, Catherine invited her mentor to lunch. When all the plates had been cleared, something still sat on the table: the questions of why she had been passed over and what her future potential would be in the new environment.

Never one to mince words, the president leaned into the table and looked her straight in the eye. "This is completely off the record. And if anyone asks me whether I said this, I'll deny it. But you should know, the reason you weren't given the job is that the management team of our new business partner doesn't think a woman could be respected in a top leadership position."

They may have called it the New Economy, but some things apparently were not all that new. Catherine was devastated. This was an insurmountable obstacle to achieving her career goals. Her dreams of dot-com millions faded away in an instant. And with those dreams, so faded her confidence.

>>> *Maintain your confidence in the face of disappointments.*

The phone rang on Catherine's desk. She answered. On the other end, the new vice president asked for a series of reports on the financial efficacy of a new software implementation that she had recommended undertaking. A figure in the document she had produced seemed to have been off, throwing off all the calculations on the subsequent pages.

Catherine hung up the phone. She saw her error in the spreadsheet. An inner voice she had heard before said, "Maybe you just weren't good enough to handle the job. Maybe they made the right decision."

The fallout from the terrorist attacks of September 11, 2001, marked the beginning of the end for Catherine's company. Additional venture funding pulled out on a promised fourth round. The company dwindled to a handful of employees. Finally, Catherine was laid off.

And thus ends the story of the New Economy.

What was she going to do? Catherine's six-figure job had suddenly become a no-figure job. She would have to live on the four weeks of severance pay her company provided and her small unemployment payments.

And it wasn't just Catherine who depended on the money. Since Catherine's father had passed away, Catherine's mother lived with and was supported by her. And while her mother did receive social security income, Catherine was still paying for the vast majority of her expenses. If Catherine was unable to work in a reasonable amount of time, paying these expenses was going to become a serious problem.

But the simple fact was that Catherine was nearly fifty years old, a challenge in a normal job market, let alone the post-9/11 job market. Employers were hiring younger workers at lower salaries—if they were hiring at all. Maybe the Voice was right. What *was* she going to do?

Catherine began the depressing task of trying to find work. But because she was competing with so many qualified people looking for work, her impressive résumé sat in a pile among hundreds of others. Interviews never came. Opportunities never presented themselves.

How can a seeming disaster be the best thing that has ever happened to you?

By the time she was laid off, I had been working with Catherine for more than a year, first to help her advance in her former company and then to deal with the gender bias with the merger. Now the focus shifted to creating a new vision and plan for her next career move. During our first meeting following her layoff, I could see that she was frightened by the prospect.

"So you lost your job," I commented. "How could this be the best thing that ever happened to you?"

Catherine was silent. She had no idea how to respond to this question. And when she did respond, it was about the daunting challenges of finding a well-paying job in a depressed job market, in an even more depressed area of information technology. In fact, she never had to create a résumé in the past, as her experience was always in demand and recruiters would call her to lure her away.

I shifted the dialogue from what she knew was so to what was possible. What dream was buried deep inside her? I explained that with an inspiring vision that played to her strengths, she could realize anything she could imagine if, like Michelangelo, she could commit to that vision with confidence.

I asked her what inspired her in past jobs, in volunteer activities, in hobbies. Always the diligent worker, she considered the question. "People have always said to me that I work hard to support other people in becoming more productive. I do enjoy making a difference because then they have more time to do the things that are most important for them. So I guess that what inspires me is . . ." She paused, her voice rising into a question as she continued. "An opportunity to help others get more done more efficiently?"

"And what possibilities could you create to help others be more efficient?"

"Well, I always wanted to start my own business. I could start an administrative and technical services business. You know, bookkeeping, professional organizing, setting up local area networks, providing PC support, that sort of thing. That would help companies focus on their main business objective."

I couldn't help smiling. Catherine saw something inside herself. She had a vision of her masterpiece, even if she wouldn't admit it. And it aligned perfectly with the values and the strengths she had developed over the course of her career.

⇒⇒ *Chip away at your inner demons.* ⇐⇐

Catherine's vision was to start a business that would help others in starting their own small businesses, providing administrative and technical services that small companies might not be able to perform.

The challenges for Catherine were her commitment and confidence. I could hear it. Inside her head the Voice still questioned Catherine every step of the way. If she were going to be successful, she was going to have to find the confidence to silence the Voice.

"What do you think of when you think of starting your own business?" I asked, hoping to reveal what was undermining her.

Catherine paused. She grew quiet and blushed. "Well . . . . that I can't do it. I mean, why should I be able to do that?"

"Why shouldn't you?"

"Well . . ." Catherine stopped. Her eyes looked off to the corner of the room. She grew silent. In that silence, I could hear the Voice listing endless reasons why Catherine didn't deserve to succeed, why she wasn't qualified, why she always ended up as a failure, and how she would end up failing again.

But what I could also see was Catherine struggling to overcome its negative message. Finally, Catherine returned to my gaze. "I guess there's no real reason why. It's just that I don't think I can."

"If thinking that you can't is the only thing that's stopping you, let's see how you can change that negative self-talk to some positive reinforcement."

⇛ Reframe your thinking. ⇚

Over the course of the next few coaching calls, I worked with Catherine to reframe her thinking, to look at what was possible, not what was wrong in the here and now. I also worked with her to recognize the Voice when it started its daily monologue, to put what it was saying in its place, to reframe its words in a more positive light or to listen to it and just laugh.

It was not an impossible task. It was simply one that required vigilance. As Catherine passed through the various tasks in starting her business, she would encounter the Voice pushing against her each step of the way, impeding her progress. Catherine and I would meet, and I would inquire about what the Voice was saying. It even got to the point where we would get together and Catherine would start in without my asking.

Each time, we'd discuss ways of reframing the negative thoughts the Voice was planting in her mind. When the Voice said she was taking too big a risk, we reframed the thought to be that she would also be taking a big risk if she didn't. When the Voice said she wouldn't find any clients, we considered all the potential clients that she already knew and wouldn't need to find. When the Voice worried about her and her mother's financial future, we considered that future rationally and worked out a budget and a plan.

All in all, we worked together to develop Catherine's confident commitment, the fire in her eyes, the faith that she could overcome any obstacle that arose.

She had come a long way. She had developed a business plan. She had settled on a company name. Logos, stationery, business cards, and computers were all in place. But there on the table, the documents of incorporation waited for her signature. Catherine paused and drew a deep breath. It was the perfect opportunity for the Voice to take center stage.

The monologue began. "Last chance, before you sign away the rest of your life to failure. Don't mind me, but I'm just saying what we both know. Everything you touch goes the way of the dinosaurs. Just look at all the companies you've worked for. Oh wait, you can't look at them. Because they don't exist anymore. Hmmm. Wonder how this one's going to turn out for you. One word: bankruptcy!"

Catherine leaned back in her chair as the monologue continued, watching the Voice on its stage like it was some third-rate insult comic in a Catskills resort. And she laughed.

Catherine collected herself and picked up the pen. With a flourish she signed the papers. Catherine was now the owner of a business, and she was committed to her vision.

"Success," she recalled someone saying, "doesn't come to you; you go to it." Now she was ready to make that journey—one that, as we will see later, was replete with promises and pitfalls.

Michelangelo Versus Leonardo

It takes great confidence to go head-to-head with the very best. You have to believe fully in your vision and be willing to lay it out for all to see. You have to know that you deserve to be in the same ring as the champ. Like Rocky. Like Michelangelo.

But here's the difference. Rocky knew he couldn't beat Apollo Creed. He just wanted to finish on his feet. Michelangelo, on the other hand, believed himself to be at least as good as the champ. Even better.

There was no question who was the champion painter in Renaissance Italy at the turn of the sixteenth century. Leonardo da Vinci was forty-eight years old and at the height of his powers. He had already painted one of the greatest frescoes of all time, *The Last Supper*, as well as more than a dozen other masterpieces, including *The Adoration of the Magi, Madonna of the Rocks*, and *Lady with an Ermine*. He was just three years from beginning work on perhaps the most fascinating painting of all time, the *Mona Lisa*.

On the other hand, at the turn of the century, Michelangelo, twenty-five years old, was considered a master sculptor and draftsman but had no great paintings to his credit. Nevertheless, he envisioned himself to be a great painter, if he chose to follow that path. And the opportunity to compete one-on-one with the great master himself was too much to let pass.

⇒≫ Seek opportunities to display your talents. ≪⇐

The opportunity came with the expansion of the Great Council Hall in Florence. The decoration of the great hall was intended to glorify Florence with depictions of two historic battles to be painted as frescoes on separate long walls. In 1503 Leonardo was invited to paint the battle at Anghiari, in which Florence had defeated the Milanese. Leonardo chose to show the ferocity of war, with lunging horses and shouting men and the patriotic struggle to retain the battle flag during hand-to-hand combat.

No one had yet been selected for the other wall. The Signoria, Florence's governing body, was seeking an artist with patriotic fervor and artistic genius. In May 1504 Michelangelo completed his sculptural masterpiece, *David*, to serve as a symbol of the Florentine Republic. Leonardo served on the committee that determined to place the great statue directly in front of the Palazzo della Signoria itself. Three months later, the Signoria decided to give Michelangelo the opportunity to paint the other council hall wall, facing Leonardo's.

Michelangelo's commission was to depict the battle of Cascina, at which Florence defeated the Pisans in 1364. Michelangelo's approach to the subject was totally different from that of Leonardo. Michelangelo chose a moment when Florence's soldiers, while bathing in the Arno River, received orders to come to battle. It would be a moment of anticipation and dramatic tension, not unlike his statue of David at the moment of anticipation of his battle with Goliath. But this scene would be replete with activity, as soldiers in various states of disarray raised the warning, signaling toward the battlefield, lumbering out of the water, and helping each other into their battle dress.

The preparatory drawings of Leonardo and Michelangelo created a great deal of excitement. Artists came from all over Italy to view them. It seemed for a while that both Michelangelo and Leonardo would be painting their frescoes simultaneously. But the epic conclusion to this competition was never to be. While Michelangelo was constructing his scaffolding and Leonardo was beginning to apply plaster and paint to the wall, an order arrived from the recently elected Pope Julius II, who had a different agenda. Michelangelo was to immediately embark for Rome to construct a massive monument including more than forty statues, which would serve as Julius's tomb.

Leonardo never finished his fresco either because an attempted innovation backfired. An oil binder he was using to enable him to paint more deliberately didn't take properly, and his fresco started to peel off the wall. While he was considering how to fix it, he was summoned to Milan by the French governor; he never resumed the painting.

>>> *Commit to your vision with confidence,
and your rewards will follow.* <<<

While the competition did not generate the expected fresco masterpieces, the drawings themselves influenced generations of artists. Raphael, for example, studied Michelangelo's drawings and committed them to memory and began to draw nude figures in the style of Michelangelo.

Michelangelo's confidence in himself was rewarded as his fame as an artist grew. And when, three years later, the pope had to decide whose talent and vision to entrust with the vast ceiling of the Sistine Chapel, only one name came to mind: Michelangelo.

Brendan

On the morning of September 11, 2001, Brendan was running late to his job as assistant controller for a securities trading company located in the North Tower of the World Trade Center. His train had stopped two stations before the final stop at the World Trade Center. He recalled, "I'll never forget—someone on the subway platform said there was a bomb scare. I walked upstairs anyway, and the first thing I noticed was debris all over the street. Up the street there was a cube of something about four feet square that once was someone's desk just sitting there. When I looked up I couldn't see the building—only smoke." Stunned, he automatically had begun to make his way to work just as he had done for the past year and a half, when a policeman stopped him and said, "Turn around—go home."

"I won't be able to get to my office at the World Trade Center?" he asked. The policeman adamantly replied, "Turn around and go home. Just go back the way you came." Brendan walked back to the train station and was able to get back to his apartment in Brooklyn. Usually he had a clear view of his office tower from his apartment terrace. Now he watched, mesmerized, seeing only black smoke billowing against the bright blue sky. The TV and Internet were useless—the transmitting antennas were on the World Trade Center.

His wife, Kelly, finally arrived home looking exhausted and disheveled, not at all the calm, impeccably dressed woman she'd been that morning. When she'd heard about the World Trade Center, she had tried to reach her husband's cell phone, but it wasn't working. By the time she left a client at City Hall to make her way home, no trains or buses were running and no taxis were to be found. So she had walked in high heels to their apartment, praying the whole time that her husband of eighteen months had escaped the devastation. When she found him home and alive, they just held each other. They climbed the stairs to look at what had been a beautiful view of the skyline. It began to sink in. Both towers were gone, and thousands of people had lost their lives in the now-smoldering rubble of what was once a mighty symbol of American ingenuity and industry. Brendan could have been one of those who perished. As he stared into the smoke-filled twilight skies over the southern tip of Manhattan, he contemplated the fragility of human life and his own mortality. How many men and women who worked in those buildings would never live to get married, have children and see them grow up, or realize their life dreams? In fact, life in New York City was going to be very different. Brendan didn't realize that in just a few weeks, his own life was going to be very different as well.

I first met Brendan in the chaotic weeks immediately following that terrorist attack. Some of the coaches from our professional association who volunteered to talk with employees of displaced World Trade Center companies had training in grief counseling or therapy. Most, including me, did not, but we were trained to be empathetic listeners and referred people to the grief counseling specialists when needed. Miraculously, all of the people in Brendan's company escaped physical injury. Many, however, would carry emotional scars. Brendan was shaken but pragmatic. He said, "I guess there is some magic in that I came close to dying and didn't. Yes, I'm furious at those who did this, but I have to keep going." Soon his direction would change 180 degrees.

>>> *Life is a fragile gift; commit to fully participate in it.* <<<

A few weeks later I got a call from Brendan for coaching assistance. He was planning to leave his company, now relocated to Jersey City, and he wanted me to work with him on creating a new career path.

We met in my office, and Brendan began to explain his dilemma. "I work for a great company—they really looked after everyone after the towers fell. But I realized I wanted a job with more human contact. Even before the attacks, I felt I couldn't stay in accounting—it was too cold and impersonal. September 11 helped me to realize that life is fragile and I don't know how much time I have left to do whatever it is I was meant to do."

His wife was presented with an opportunity to become the senior legal counsel for a Fortune 500 company located in a small town in northern Connecticut. This created a natural break for Brendan. He had already had two careers, first as a professionally trained cook, which he found too financially insecure, and then as an accountant, which was personally unsatisfying. He wanted to brainstorm with me ideas for a new career.

Brendan first wanted to consider starting his own business, perhaps a hobby shop—a place that could enable parents and their children to spend time together. "As a kid, I loved to share hobbies with my father," Brendan said. "Dad and I would spend hours in the basement with our Lionel train set, building villages, adding new track, and painting scenery. Sometimes my friends and their fathers joined us, and we'd all have an incredible time. Primarily, though, it was all about spending time with my father.

"To me, my dad was the greatest man who ever lived, but he was never given any real opportunities in his life. He worked at terrible jobs his whole life. He was a stevedore, loading and unloading ships on the docks. But he was smart and strong. He had a toughness that you don't see anymore. Watching him was like watching Humphrey Bogart or Jimmy Cagney in a movie. He wasn't really the macho type, just a really tough guy with quiet strength. He needed to be tough to survive as an Irish immigrant trying to provide for his family in New York City. I think that he was trying to be the father he himself never had." Brendan could no longer conceal his tears. "He was diagnosed with cancer when he was fifty-five, and he was gone in six months. I was twenty-five. I wish I could have had more time with him."

>>> *Be prepared to shift gears without losing steam.* <<<

Brendan and I met together for several sessions, exploring marketing, logistical, and financial issues for starting such a business in the area he was moving to. But this was not to be, at least for some time to come. Another life-changing event altered Brendan's career plans. It would be both his greatest opportunity and his greatest challenge.

Brendan and Kelly were in their mid-thirties when they married. Kelly's first pregnancy ended in miscarriage—an abnormality of the placenta, they were told, which portended a significant risk that she would develop uterine cancer. "We waited six months so that she could be monitored for signs of cancer. Finally we got the OK to try again. Less than a year later, our prayers were answered when we had Connor, our beautiful boy."

I had known about Connor. I had seen his photo on Brendan's Christmas card a few months earlier. But now I learned the details of this baby, who was such an unexpected miracle. The cherubic face and broad smile told me that this was one happy baby. Brendan's e-mails told me that he and Kelly were happy parents.

We toasted his now six-month-old boy, and Brendan shared with me the story of his new life and career as a stay-at-home dad.

"I grew up in a very traditional family," he began. "My mother was always home when we got back from school. My father was the sole source of income. I never expected Kelly to be the wage earner while I'm the stay-at-home parent."

I asked Brendan if he was comfortable in his new role. "At first I was very troubled by it. You've got to remember that my dad was my role model and that he worked on the docks. For him, to be a man meant you had to be strong, and to be strong meant you had to be the breadwinner. And somewhere deep down that's a part of me."

Don't be wedded to your childhood impressions.

"But times have changed, and over the years things have happened to me that have shaken that view. A number of years ago I was dating a real estate broker. In her high-earning years, when housing was strong, she earned a lot more than me. She loved doing special things, like going to expensive restaurants and luxury hotels when we traveled, and paying for both of us. I was very reluctant to let her pay my share but gave in after she repeatedly insisted. The housing market collapsed at the same time as my earnings as an accountant were rising. Even though our financial situations had reversed, she refused to let me pay for the extras. She would rather do without them. I thought a lot about that. For her, money was power, and whoever had it within the relationship was in charge. I knew that a part of me responded to that same feeling, and I was determined not to allow it to govern my relationships. That idea has really helped me accept being an at-home dad.

"The more I think about and experience being an at-home dad, the more comfortable I've become. It goes back to the values that I learned as a child from my mother. I was taught that who you are as a person is more important than what you do for a living or how much you make doing it.

"I think that the man's role in the family is to do the right thing for his family," he added. "You have to do whatever your family needs most. I learned that from my dad. And if my wife makes enough so that I don't need to work, then the right thing for me to do is to be here and raise my child. On some level I'll probably continue to be uncomfortable that I'm not the breadwinner. But the way I see it my job now is to make sure that my son will grow up to be a successful, thoughtful, intelligent, and well-mannered person who, when given a choice, will always choose the right action."

"What is it like to be at home with your child?" I asked.

Brendan reflected for a moment. "Now I have a short, bald, demanding boss who speaks a language I can't understand but manages to let me know that I just can't get it right—just like a certain German chef I worked for as a cook," he responded with a laugh.

"Do you feel prepared for this job?" I asked.

"Well, a few of the mothers I have met along the way have at times shown, either by word or by deed, that they think I don't know what I'm doing. Being criticized by someone outside of your life is really difficult for anyone, and I can only imagine these women would never offer some of the stupid comments they have offered me to another woman. Sometimes getting it right with the little man is hard, but I'm a quick learner. As for being the domestic spouse, well, I used to joke that with degrees in cooking and accounting, I was going to make someone a wonderful wife someday," he said, as we shared another good laugh.

"I knew from an early age that I wanted to be a father," Brendan recalled, "though I almost lost the chance. My father and my grand-father worked jobs that most people wouldn't touch in order to give their children the best education and opportunities in life. With Connor I am passing the torch from one generation to the next. I was fortunate to marry not just the best woman I ever met but the best *person* I ever met. And she is sharing with me the responsibility of raising and providing for our child.

"Kelly and I have talked very openly about our roles as parents," Brendan went on. "We decided to expose Connor to as many experiences and ideas as we can and to watch carefully to see what sparks his interest. And then to help him nurture that passion so that he can develop and grow into the rarest of men and do something for a living that he really cares about."

I asked, "Does Kelly ever feel that she is missing out on anything since you are the stay-at-home parent and she's not?"

After a pause, Brendan replied, "Yes, she would like to spend as much time with the little man as I do. But she understands that right now the way we have structured things is best for Connor. And that's what is most important to her."

"What's life going to be like for you when Connor is in school?" I inquired.

"I might buy a hobby shop. Or I may just wind up taking Conner to soccer practice. It may be that I just keep doing what I'm doing now up through high school. Kelly and I have a contract with each other. My mother and father each had a clear understanding of what each person had to do. And Kelly and I are clear about what our strengths are in this family."

Brendan knew he could properly raise Connor. He had a vision of what he wanted his child to become and how he wanted to nurture him. And, despite living in a world vastly different from the one in which he grew up, Brendan had confidence that the tools he had been given by his loving parents would provide him with the strength and wisdom to care for his child.

⇒⇒ *Take advantage of what fate unexpectedly offers you.* ⇐⇐

Sometimes unexpected events and challenges turn our lives off course, leaving us with no way of knowing where these changes will lead. Michelangelo confidently accepted the change in role from sculptor to painter to compete with Leonardo in producing frescoes for Florence's new council hall. The famous drawings that resulted greatly enhanced Michelangelo's reputation as a painter, perhaps earning for him the right to paint one of the world's great masterpieces on the ceiling of the Sistine Chapel. After the September 11 attacks, Brendan left accounting to become an at-home dad, a difficult role reversal for someone who had always thought of himself as a breadwinner. But he took on this role with confidence, which grew each day as he saw his son develop and thrive under his care.

Brendan's current journey is not over, and there are sure to be new challenges ahead. But he is convinced that Connor will be his most important legacy. And isn't a well-loved child a kind of masterpiece?

Sculpt Your Personal Masterpiece

Once you've aligned your personal values, passions, and strengths to envision your masterpiece, the road may not run smoothly from your door to an extraordinary life. There may be more than a few bumps and turns along the way. There might not even be blacktop!

Success in realizing your masterpiece requires committing to your vision no matter what stands in the way. It also means harnessing the inner will to overcome all the obstacles that will inevitably lie in your path. Have the faith that "you can" and "you will." Commit to your vision with confidence.

Michelangelo showed commitment with confidence in maintaining his focus in light of his father's strong objections. When his father said "you can't" or "you won't," Michelangelo knew that "he could" and "he would." Michelangelo never gave in to self-doubt.

At one time or another, we've all heard our own inner voice, that negative self-talk that chips away at our faith. At our darkest moments that Voice can become a rather sarcastic, defeatist enemy. But if we are going to truly commit with confidence, we must find a way to ring down the curtain on the Voice and replace it with the sound of our will.

Finding our will can sometimes be difficult. But if we remain focused on our vision and maintain a positive attitude, it is possible.

When you hear the Voice, replace its negativity with empowering questions. Change its words to your will. Ask yourself these questions:

+ What will my life be like when I get what I want?

+ How can I take responsibility for creating the life of my dreams?

* How can I overcome the gaps and roadblocks to my success?

* How can I reframe, or view, this next task so that I will overcome this seemingly insurmountable obstacle?

Above all else, hold the sight of the masterpiece inside you. Be confident. It's there, waiting for you to uncover it. And it will be revealed. It will just take time and effort. Commit with confidence, and you will be unstoppable.

Discovery Exercises

1. Pick three areas or situations in which you usually hear the Voice. For instance, in work meetings, at social gatherings, or when you are laying in bed at night. Over a period of a week, carry around a notebook and write down any self-talk you experience in these areas. List the triggers for this self-talk and any negative behavior or actions that resulted.

2. Now decide how you might reframe your self-talk in a way to create positive behaviors. For instance, reframe "I'd love to have that, but I could never afford it" to "I'd love to have that, and I will work hard to ensure that I get it."

3. Write down the positive behaviors that could have resulted if you hadn't heeded the Voice. List the benefits of silencing the Voice.

4. For the next week, continue to record the times when you hear the Voice and what you did to reframe your thinking or silence the Voice. What were the benefits you experienced?

Pietà

This was the only work that Michelangelo signed. He did so because he was relatively unknown at the time, and he over-heard people attributing the masterpiece to another artist. The *Pietà*, which gained him wide acclaim, exemplifies the Renaissance ideals of truth, beauty, and harmony.

Photograph by Ron Paxton

5

Plan First, Then Chip Away

After completing many detailed sketches, Michelangelo was ready to go to a three-dimensional figure in clay. Here he would have free expression because the material could be moved to distort form. Next he turned to wax because there was a similarity of wax to marble in tactile quality and translucence. Yet he never allowed these models to become fixed in his mind; they remained rough starting points. The true surge had to be inside the marble itself.

—The Story of Michelangelo's Pietà,
Irving Stone, 1964

Planning requires the right materials to work with. Garbage in, garbage out, as they say in the computer world. And therein lies the rub. Most people lose the opportunity to create their personal masterpiece after the first rush of inspiration. They forget that they can usually go only as far as their materials will take them. Sometimes your material is your body, sometimes your mind, sometimes your equipment, and sometimes the circumstances in which you find yourself. People are so anxious to begin the journey that they forget to plan for their resources. Michelangelo knew this, and so he planned to get the most perfect piece of marble he could find.

Take, for example, Michelangelo's *Pietà*. This life-size statue, depicting Mary holding the dead Christ, was commissioned by a cardinal for placement at his own tomb in St. Peter's Basilica in Rome. Michelangelo was intent on creating a masterpiece.

For this project he determined he would need a very large block of white marble—seven feet wide, six feet high, and three feet deep. He searched throughout Rome and all the ports in the area but could find nothing that met his high standards. So Michelangelo carefully considered his options and decided to travel to Carrara, more than two hundred miles away, where the finest marble in Italy was to be found. There, on the slopes of an ancient quarry, he discovered the block he needed.

Michelangelo, though, was only partway to obtaining the marble for his *Pietà*. Now he had to devise a plan to transport this huge slab back to Rome without damaging it in the process. Only twenty-three years old at the time and inexperienced in moving large pieces of stone, he decided that he would need help from someone he could trust. So he traveled sixty miles across the mountains to Florence to visit his family and to secure the services of an old family friend and experienced stoneworker, Michele di Piero Pippo, who accompanied him back to Carrara.

To get the block to Rome in one piece, Michelangelo's friend advised him to ship it by sea. The artist had the block rough hewn, hauled down the steep slopes leading from the quarry to the sea, and loaded on a ship for transport to Rome. The shipment was then held in port until a new duty imposed on marble exports could be paid. Finally, the gorgeous block of white marble arrived in Rome, intact, seven months after Michelangelo had first set out for Carrara.

⇒⟩ *Follow your critical path.* ⟨⇐

Planning does not mean taking the easiest route. It means finding the path necessary to get you to your goal and having the determination to follow that path all the way to its end. And some elements of every plan are more important than others. You need to decide what those elements are and make sure you implement them carefully. For Michelangelo, the quality of the marble that he wanted to use for his *Pietà* was of fundamental importance. There were no shortcuts to be found between Rome and Carrara. Michelangelo made the full effort and in doing so made possible the creation of his timeless masterpiece.

Five years after completing his widely acclaimed *Pietà*, Michelangelo began an even more daunting project, the tomb of Pope Julius II. As originally conceived, the tomb was to include more than forty statues. The centerpiece would ultimately be another of Michelangelo's great masterpieces, his *Moses*, which stunned and awed his contemporaries. As Vasari, an accomplished artist in his own right, put it, "No other modern work will ever bear comparison; nor, indeed, do the statues of the ancient world. Michelangelo expressed in marble the divinity that God first infused in Moses' most holy form. Every part of the work is finished so expertly that [visitors] will be adoring something that is divine rather than human." Legend has it that Michelangelo himself was so overwhelmed by the masterpiece that he threw his chisel at the statue while imploring, "Why don't you talk?" causing a chip in the knee that is visible today.

Looking at the massive slab of rock from which *Moses* was to be sculpted, Michelangelo envisioned a physically powerful Moses holding under his right arm the tablet of the Ten Commandments, seated in an attitude of deep thought and wisdom, his face capable of inspiring both love and fear. Seeing the inspiring leader of the Jews inside that stone required incredible insight. But even with vision, the hard work had just begun. For working in stone poses its own set of challenges, because no two blocks of stone are alike. Each chunk of marble is vastly different in color, in texture, in pattern, and in hardness.

You might say that each stone has its own unique masterpiece trapped inside it.

⋙ *It's all there, deep inside—a masterpiece imprisoned.* ⋘

Imagine again that you're Michelangelo standing before the huge stone in which he saw his *Moses* trapped. There you are, taking in the stone. You're determined to fulfill your commission and create a symbol worthy of the tomb of your benefactor, the Supreme Pontiff of the Universal Church, Pope Julius II.

Now look at the slab before you. There, deep in its recesses is your vision, your *Moses*—seated, his head turned, his shoulders bold and square, his eyes focused in the distance.

It's all there deep inside this marble, a masterpiece imprisoned. And you can set it free.

⋙ *Think before you act.* ⋘

Michelangelo, flush with his vision, could have plunged head-first into the work and fallen to the stone's challenges. He could have struck his hammer and chisel feverishly without planning his strikes. He could have allowed his passion to override all his knowledge of stone and all the skill of his hands. In short, Michelangelo could have let his vision blind him to what was directly in front of him.

But Michelangelo did nothing of the sort. What he did do was proceed methodically according to a careful plan.

First, Michelangelo studied the huge block of stone. Rather than focusing on imposing his vision on the stone, Michelangelo envisioned what was inherently in the crystalline structure of the stone and allowed the stone's particular temperament to dictate the work of revealing that vision.

But before he picked up his hammer there was still more planning to do. Michelangelo made hundreds of sketches detailing each part of the statue. He then followed his sketching by creating models in clay and wax. Then, finally satisfied with these models, Michelangelo picked up his chisel and mallet and prepared to strike the first blow.

And prepared he was. For Michelangelo planned thoroughly first and then chipped away.

As his hammer met the chisel with a resounding clang, and as the first chunk of marble flew from the stone, if you put your eye to the fracture and peered deep inside, you just might see what Michelangelo already saw. You just might see Moses ready to be free.

⇒ *Plan first, then chip away.* ⇐

When we glimpse our future selves, it's hard not to rush headlong into changing our lives. The excitement of holding a vision can make us restless. Like a child on the night before Christmas, we can't sleep knowing that downstairs presents wait under the tree.

Sometimes, this feeling of anxious expectation can make our current situation unbearable. If we can see the other life we want so clearly, why can't we just live it right now? Sometimes we make the rash decision to go ahead and do just that. We attempt to move forward, to live the life we want without planning the correct path to get it or, worse, without fully understanding the contours of our vision. This leads to the worst possible outcome. We fail to achieve our vision.

Ben

Remember Ben, the investment banker from Chapter 1? After Ben and I met for the first few times, I could see he was growing excited. And how could he not be? Ben had been deeply unhappy working in investment banking. Even large bonus checks weren't enough compensation for the long hours away from his family. And until we met, it all seemed hopeless to him. But then Ben looked inside himself and saw the outline of a masterpiece—a career that would express his passions and values.

Frankly, Ben didn't really know exactly what the details of his masterpiece entailed. All he had glimpsed was the shadow of its outline in the stone. But as uncertain as he felt about his vision, he knew he wanted to reveal it immediately. So, rashly, Ben made a decision. He was about to discover that you can't just chip away without a proper plan and get directly to your vision.

The worst part of Ben's investment banking lifestyle was his work schedule. On average Ben worked more than eighty hours a week. And worse, Ben could never predict when he would be needed. His life was defined by the deals he was working on and the managing partners' schedules. So Ben could forget about planning to be there for his daughter's birthday party, to celebrate his anniversary, or to go on a family vacation. On a moment's notice, he might have to break whatever plans had been made, no matter how important they were to him or his family.

⇢⇥ *Don't let your hopes obscure the truth.* ⇤⇠

"Maybe if I had a more flexible work schedule," Ben thought to himself, "I would find my way to my masterpiece. Maybe I can create the flexibility I need while continuing as an investment banker."

Soon Ben convinced himself that all he needed to do was have a talk with the managing director for assignments, Andre Worthington.

When Ben hit his desk at 8 A.M. the next morning, he made the call to Worthington. At the tone he left the message. "It's Ben. I'm hoping I can get into your schedule today. I have a few things I'd appreciate discussing with you."

An hour later he got the call from Worthington's assistant. The meeting was on for 3 P.M.

All day Ben ran his meetings at warp speed. Over a business lunch, he watched the conversation as if he were dining at another table. He could already feel himself slowly moving outside this world of mergers and acquisitions. He cut into his steak and took a bite. It tasted better.

When it came time for his meeting with Worthington, Ben practically jumped from his chair. At 3 P.M. on the dot, Ben opened the heavy oak door that led to the office of the managing director and partner.

"Have a seat," Worthington offered. Ben took the chair with relish.

And so, Ben pitched his proposal. He laid out how difficult it was for him to balance his professional and his personal life. He said that he was satisfied with his compensation and his title, but he needed more flexibility.

When Ben finished, Worthington's fingers drummed the table. His eyes looked off into the apparently more contemplative reaches of his office. Ben felt his own palms starting to sweat. Something was awry.

Finally, Worthington's gaze returned to Ben. "Look, Ben, I completely understand your problem. It's not so uncommon at all for people just starting out in this field. But take it from me. When you decide to enter the world of investment banking, you don't just buy into your salary package, you buy into the total package. With the expense accounts, bonuses, and private jets, you also get a lack of personal time.

"It's a hard adjustment, I know. I went through it myself. And we have ways of helping you through the transition. We all value your work around here. I'm sure we can figure something out that will work for you. I'll talk to the other partners."

>>> *Be realistic as to what you can expect from others.* <<<

Two weeks later, Ben received more money in his paycheck and, with it, a new box of business cards. When he opened the box, he realized that he had received a promotion—but no change in his work schedule. He began to feel that he was in an episode of "The Twilight Zone." Ben decided he would have to leave investment banking.

Everywhere Ben went, when he mentioned the possibility of leaving investment banking, people looked at him like he was crazy. His mentor and the smartest person he knew, Peter Simon, suggested that he stay two more years "to learn the business." At cocktail parties people would look at him like he'd been drinking too much. Then they looked for an excuse to leave him. Even his daughter got into the act. One night while sitting down at dinner, his daughter asked him how much money he would make if he remained an investment banker. When Ben quoted her a possible figure, she gasped. "Dad, it's OK if I don't see you a lot. I'd rather be rich!"

Ben began to doubt his decision. If so many people couldn't understand what he was doing, how could he understand it himself? Maybe he was making the wrong choice. He closed his eyes and looked inside himself. He tried to look deep inside for his vision of who he could be. All he could see now was rough, unworked stone.

⤞ *Are you being true to your vision?* ⤝

When Ben arrived at my doorstep, he was a confused man. "I don't understand what's happening. I have my vision. I'm committed to making a change. But now I'm thinking that maybe I've made the wrong decision."

"Why do you think that you've made the wrong decision?"

"Because everyone I mention it to looks at me like I'm crazy. Especially my colleagues. Some of them think that I'm a quitter. That I can't take the pressure of the big leagues."

"Well, I don't think that's true. Look, when we began working together, it was clear to both of us what was important to you. More than anything, you value your family. And we both know you're passionate about making a positive difference in the lives of others. And all of that is still true, isn't it?"

"Yes."

"Then the only question you have to ask yourself is if you are being true to your vision for yourself if you remain an investment banker."

"I could certainly donate a lot of money to charities!"

I laughed. "Sure. And you could buy your wife a great anniversary gift and pay for your daughter's education in cash. And there is nothing wrong with that. But would that be enough? Living rich is one thing. Living richly is another."

"It would be nice to have both."

"Who says you can't? Let's work on that. How could you do what you love and have financial rewards?"

"Now that's the million-dollar question."

"And the million-dollar answer is inside you. What you need to do is plan carefully and come up with a strategy to reveal it. Then we can chip away at everyone else's expectations and get down to what you need. Once we do that—and you have to trust me on this—you will find the answer you're looking for."

⟫ Keep your plan simple, prioritized, and focused. ⟪

That night Ben locked himself in his home office and turned on his stereo. Bob Dylan rolled from the speakers. "The answer, my friends, is blowin' in the wind." Well, maybe not the wind, Ben smiled. He pulled a blank sheet of paper from his desk and began to sketch a plan.

His plan was a simple one. First, Ben recognized that for a while he would have to work even harder than before while he handled his current responsibilities and tried to open up new job opportunities. But in the long run the sacrifice would be worth it. After all, he knew what he was sacrificing for: his vision.

The first task Ben set down for his free time was to make a list of ventures that might interest him.

He stared at a blank sheet of paper. "Well, I had always been interested in real estate." It wasn't a passing fancy; real estate was a true strength of Ben's. In fact, his main projects as the state's development commissioner had been real estate projects: waterfront development and redevelopment of declining industrial areas.

So, real estate went on the top of his list.

Ben followed real estate with "returning to government," "not-for-profit organizations," and "financial officer of a major corporation."

⫸ *Think creatively in developing your plan.* ⫷

Ben looked long and hard at his list. It was then that he had a realization. "If I did something entrepreneurial," he thought, "I could have maximum control and create the time I want with my family."

Ben was onto something. His planning suddenly moved into fifth gear. He began to look forward to the work of figuring out what he was to do next. He even began to carry in his back pocket a notebook for jotting down his ideas.

Next, Ben reviewed his investment banking assignments to see if any of his current deals could help him achieve one of these goals. One project seemed particularly promising. Ben had recently been assigned to sell a California-based real estate development company. He determined he should focus as much time as possible on understanding the company's business operations.

Real estate was quickly becoming more of a focus for Ben. Even with his experience in urban development, Ben knew he could never have enough knowledge. So he considered enrolling in a course in development being given at a local university. This proved to be a dead end, for his work constraints made that commitment impossible. Not to be discouraged, Ben took himself to the public library and created his own reading list of articles and books about real estate development, particularly development that aided the poor.

In his notebook, Ben also made a long list of all potential contacts he could network with for potential jobs. There were nearly one hundred names in all. In addition, he began scouring the *New York Times* for available positions in both the public and corporate sectors.

➢➢➢ *Concentrate on your best personal contacts.*

One summer day, Ben was playing Frisbee in Central Park with his daughter, Tessa. The Frisbees flew back and forth. As Ben tossed one to his daughter, he caught sight of the New York City skyline across the park. As he looked at the buildings, a name popped into his head. "How did I forget Jeff?"

Across the lawn, Tessa caught the toss, spun round, and quickly sent a perfect throw her dad's way. The Frisbee spiraled high across the Great Lawn. Right to Ben. And right over his head.

"Dad! You missed it!"

"Sorry. I had to jot down a name." Ben put his notebook back in his pocket and scooped up the Frisbee. It spun around in the sky like a satellite headed straight for the stars.

The name Ben wrote in his notebook that day—Jeff, his former college roommate and still a very close friend—turned out to be the most important one. When Ben called Jeff, it turned out he was also looking for a new job.

Jeff, a lawyer, had been head of the real estate division of the Department of Public Advocacy in a neighboring state, where he had been particularly successful in litigating on behalf of the needs of low-income families and senior citizens. With a new, more conservative governor coming into office, one who promised smaller budgets for social programs, Jeff's days were clearly numbered.

So Jeff was trying to put together a private company that could take advantage of opportunities to enlist private enterprise in the creation of low-income housing. He had already selected a planner, Frank, but needed a business partner. A lunch was definitely in order.

Over lunch in Central Park, Ben and Jeff caught up on old times and then began to talk about their mutual visions. When they realized they had a shared mission in life, the conversation became animated and deeply meaningful. By the time they finished lunch, the sun was setting over the New York skyline. It seems Jeff had found his third partner. And Ben had found the key to freeing his vision.

⇛ *Call upon your experience in implementing your plan.* ⇚

Of course, the idea of a company would have to be turned into reality. As the business partner, this would be largely Ben's responsibility. He needed to create a business plan, something with which he was very familiar. But to do so, he again needed to find the time.

Ben discussed this with his wife, Amanda, who had been so supportive of his need to take time to plan for his vision. Now, while trying to get this company started, he would have even less free time than before. But she agreed that it was better to begin work on it now so that the company would be up and running when he left investment banking.

With summer being a bit slower, Ben was able to work many nights and finalize a business plan, which he, Jeff, and Frank could use to raise capital for the new venture. Ben's vision was off and running. His confidence swelled. He understood the next steps and realized that his masterpiece was in his hands.

The next week Ben gave official notice. In three months, he would complete the deals he was working on and leave the world of investment banking.

⇛ *Don't be deterred by the negative reactions of others.* ⇚

Suddenly, Ben's status around the office changed. He was no longer seen as the rising talent and future partner. Now he was seen as someone getting out. The change was even more perceptible than before when Ben had begun to tell people he had second thoughts about his career as an investment banker. Whereas people before were less interested in talking to him about the politics of the office or changes at competitor firms, now Ben was entirely excluded from the conversation. He had become an outsider.

One day Ben arrived home after a difficult day at the office. That particular evening there was an office gathering at a local bar celebrating the retirement of one of the older partners in the firm. Despite not being close to this partner, Ben had wanted to go. Even though his colleagues had come to see him as an outsider, it would still be good to bond with them, now that he'd made this decision. After all, who knew how important these relationships would be to his future?

When Ben looked at his schedule, however, he saw every hour blocked out for the week. And tonight was the only time he could spend with his family. Considering how little time he had had for them over the past few months, he couldn't tolerate passing that up.

Ben hailed a cab and directed the driver to his home.

As Ben rode home in the cab up Park Avenue, he looked up at the steel towers that stood along both sides of the wide street, each a testament to the power and influence of banking. Ben felt a little nostalgic as he rode. He looked up as he passed by. The towers, so tall and proud, stretching endless stories into the sky—what could be greater in life than being a part of that? Could Ben, no matter how well he planned, create something as impressive and important as what went on in these buildings?

> *A career plan is only one part of a life plan.*

Ben arrived at his building. Albert, the elevator man, opened the door for him and greeted him with a smile. Together they crossed the lobby to the elevator. Albert threw open the old steel gate of the elevator, and Ben stepped inside. Ben watched as Albert's hand gripped the elevator's throttle and began the ascent up to Ben's floor.

As they rode up the fifteen stories, Albert asked him about his day and reported to him about Tessa. "She's growing up nice and polite, just like her mamma and daddy," Albert said. "Now you have a good night, sir." Ben thanked him, and as Albert closed the door, Ben heard him whistling to himself. A happy tune no less.

"He always seemed to be whistling," Ben thought. "He always seemed to be smiling, too. What does he have to be happy about?" Ben wondered.

Here was someone who spent his whole day at the service of other people, all much more well-to-do than he was. He ironed his uniform each morning and spent each day opening and closing the doors of an old Otis elevator. He was often ignored as he polished the brass or drove residents deep in conversation with their friends, spouses, or lovers to their floors. He accepted their packages and delivered them. He helped old people down the stairs of the lobby. How could this man be happy, considering he spent most of his day doing routine tasks for people who didn't really know him?

And yet there he was, still whistling.

In fact, he did make a difference in the lives of residents in the building. When a teenage babysitter staying with Tessa tried to have her boyfriend come upstairs, Albert wouldn't permit it. One day Ben overheard an eight-year-old, whose mother was late arriving home from work, say to a friend, "I can't leave the lobby. My elevator man won't let me." He protected and cared about the people in the building. And the residents cared about him. Though low in status in the world's eyes, he believed his job was important. Albert knew who he was.

And surely, Albert had his own dreams. Who's to say he wasn't living them? He probably had every reason to be happy, possibly more reason than Ben did in the world of investment banking.

Ben swore he could hear him whistling the whole way down. Ben joined the tune.

Ben was still whistling as he opened the door to his apartment. He had come home.

Sculpt Your Personal Masterpiece

You believe it—there's a masterpiece inside your stone. And you've got the strengths to reveal it. You're even committed to it with confidence. But how do you begin to make your masterpiece a reality? How do you start to break through to your extraordinary life?

If you're pondering these questions, you're off to a great start. Taking the right steps at the beginning is key. When you're creating a masterpiece as Michelangelo did with his *Pietà*, you can't simply pull out a hammer, eagerly smash away, and expect everything to fall into place. You must plan first and then chip away carefully.

As we know, what made Michelangelo such a successful sculptor was his ability to plan methodically. Starting with drawings, moving to clay and then to wax models, and still not breaking stone until he understood the characteristics of the stone before him, Michelangelo planned very carefully before he started his work.

Likewise, if you want your extraordinary life to come to reality, you, too, must plan. Without planning, you might find yourself on the wrong track. Maybe you'll achieve some movement, but not in the direction you want to go!

Planning first keeps you on the right track toward your vision. Having a plan allows you to monitor your progress, which goals you're achieving, and which goals are still to be reached. And it announces your intentions to the world, giving you a vehicle to explain your vision and perhaps even rally help toward getting there.

Most important, creating a plan gives order to your experience of moving forward. In planning we come to understand our vision better. We see the gaps in our thinking. We find details in its articulation. We improve.

In making your plan, you have to ask yourself hard questions to define the actions you need to take. Be concrete and honest in your answers.

Ask yourself these questions:

+ What are my tasks to achieve these goals?

+ What resources will I need to realize my vision?

+ How long will it take to achieve my masterpiece?

+ What milestones along the way can help to guide me and gauge progress?

+ What support will I need to follow through?

And once you've laid out your plan and you begin to chip away, remember that a successful plan is a flexible plan. Life, after all, is unpredictable. If you are going to truly achieve your vision and make real breakthroughs in your life and career, you must roll with these twists of fate. Yes, hold your vision, but never so tightly that it crumbles.

Every so often as you proceed, review your plan and evaluate it for its effectiveness. Examine what you've accomplished to date, where you've fallen short, what's working and what isn't. Perhaps you didn't anticipate certain contingencies that necessitate additional time or resources for your efforts. Or maybe a particular task is no longer necessary.

But even if it seems as if you're making no progress, don't give up on your plan. Study it. Be clear about what you're doing and why.

Has anything changed since you began implementing the plan? Are there activities that are getting in the way of achieving your milestones? How can you work around them?

In short, if you work with your plan, your plan will work for you. No masterpiece has ever been created by accident. All great things come from great plans.

Discovery Exercises

1. List at least ten major steps you'll need to take to obtain your leading choice for an important life goal. Write down these steps in order, each on a different sheet of paper.

2. Under each of the major steps, list the tasks required to achieve the step. Prioritize them according to which task needs to precede the others. Study the steps you've written out. Are there some you can break down further? Create miniplans based on these steps. Write down your miniplans. Continue with this until you feel you've covered all the important activities required to achieve your plan.

3. Next to each task indicate who else needs to be involved in the task. What specific responsibility will you have for completing the task, and what might be delegated to others? Where you plan to delegate a task, indicate how you will monitor the progress.

4. Create a time frame for each task. Work backward from the date upon which you would like to reach your goal, allowing the necessary time for each task to be completed. If you find it is impossible to achieve your goal within the time you have allowed, revise your completion date to allow more time and redo your interme-

diate time frames. Realize that setbacks are a normal part of the process, and allow some extra time.

5. Now at the bottom of each page, list the major obstacles to achieving each of your major steps. The obstacles are the stone that you will need to chip away to reveal your extraordinary career. Some of these obstacles may be personal, like dealing with negative self-talk and peer pressure, and others may relate to areas in which you just need more experience or knowledge in order to achieve competency (for example, creating a realistic, detailed budget to finance your plan). You should frequently review tasks related to these major obstacles to assure that they are being appropriately addressed. While you are chipping away, be careful not to write your plan in stone. For your plan to be useful, it needs to be a living, flexible document, capable of being revised as circumstances change.

You now have your long-term plan. Ask yourself what steps you can begin to take today. Now is the time to start.

Tomb of Lorenzo de' Medici

The design for the tomb of Michelangelo's most ardent
patron juxtaposes the female *Dawn* on the right and
male *Evening* on the left, symbolizing Lorenzo's (and all
of humankind's) reflective and active lives—a balance of
thinking and doing.

Photograph by Ron Paxton

6

Find Your Support

Michelangelo had formed a friendship with Francesco Granacci, who, likewise a lad, had placed himself with Domenico Ghirlandaio in order to learn the art of painting. Granacci, loving Michelangelo, and perceiving that he was much inclined to design, supplied him daily with drawings by Ghirlandaio, who at that time was reputed to be one of the best masters that there was not only in Florence, but throughout Italy.
　　　　　　　　　　　　　—Life of Michelangelo,
　　　　　　　　　　　　　　Giorgio Vasari, 1568

To most people in today's world, the name Francesco Granacci means nothing. Ask for Granacci on the street, and you're more likely to be directed to the nearest Italian restaurant than you are to a museum.

Of course, say the name Michelangelo, and people immediately conjure the picture of a masterpiece in their mind—the *David*, the Sistine Chapel ceiling. Five hundred years have passed, and still everyone knows Michelangelo.

Well, most people would be shocked to know that without a certain obscure Italian Renaissance painter named Francesco Granacci, there might be no *David* and no Sistine Chapel ceiling. Because without Francesco Granacci, there might be no Michelangelo.

As we know by now, as a young boy Michelangelo was forced to hide his talent from his family. Though even at a young age Michelangelo wanted nothing more than to be an artist, his tyrannical father, Ludovico, had another vision for the boy.

One must imagine that Michelangelo spent many nights in his lonely room, silently sketching by moonlight, and many more days hiding his sketches. One must imagine that, as he hid his sketches, Michelangelo felt he was hiding himself. One must imagine he wanted desperately to be found.

➵➵ *We all want to be "discovered."* ⧽⧼

It was then that young Michelangelo met Francesco Granacci.

Michelangelo met Granacci while attending the grammar school of Master Francesco Galeota. Granacci was a budding artist himself. A few years older than young Michelangelo, he was already serving as an apprentice to the leading Florentine painter, Domenico Ghirlandaio. Granacci was not only a talented artist, but he was one who lived the life that Michelangelo saw inside himself.

Each day at the grammar school, Michelangelo showed great interest in Granacci's work. When Granacci learned of his friend's own passion for making art, he asked to view the young artist's sketches.

The next day, Michelangelo sneaked his sketches from his house. When he presented them to his friend, Granacci was struck dumb. The maturity of his line, the attention to form and structure in the rendering, the elegance of the composition—his young friend was a true artist. Why was he not an apprentice to one of the great masters?

When Granacci learned how Michelangelo's family stifled the boy's talents, Granacci took him under his wing—as an apprentice's apprentice. As Granacci learned from Ghirlandaio, copying his work to apprehend the nuance of line, Michelangelo would learn from Granacci. Each day the older boy would bring young Michelangelo his own work as well as drawings from the master Ghirlandaio for him to copy. Michelangelo's work progressed quickly. Soon that work was superior to Granacci's.

But Granacci was not jealous of his friend's talent. He was in awe. How could anyone be jealous of such rare genius? Genius, after all, was the gift of the Creator. And it should never be stifled. It must flower.

> ⇛ *To create your masterpiece,*
> *you must find the right teacher.* ⇚

But how could he, Granacci, continue to teach a genius? No, it was time. He must convince Michelangelo to enter Ghirlandaio's studio and ask to be an apprentice of the true master.

With his friend's support, Michelangelo agreed. And so, Granacci led Michelangelo to Ghirlandaio's dark studio.

As they walked in with a folder of Michelangelo's work, the other students looked up with curiosity. Granacci ignored their stares and eagerly asked his master to appraise the young boy's work, which, Granacci claimed, surpassed his own. Curious, the master painter crossed the room.

Granacci spread Michelangelo's sketches out on the cluttered drafting table. Ghirlandaio leaned over them. He studied the line in silence. Minutes passed. Finally, Ghirlandaio lifted his head from the boy's work. "Tell the boy's father he can be my apprentice."

The die was cast. Michelangelo had been liberated from his hiding place. Here was an artist! With Granacci's encouragement and support, Michelangelo would confront his father. The two boys stood together fighting for the cause of genius.

Years later, Granacci and Michelangelo continued to stand together, supporting each other as they faced new challenges. They both graduated from Ghirlandaio's studio and went on to the new school for sculpture set up by Lorenzo the Magnificent.

By the time they graduated as master sculptors, Michelangelo had become known as Florence's most promising young artist. Even as Michelangelo's fame grew, he stood with his good friend Granacci, working with him in Florence and taking him to Rome to assist on some of his greatest projects.

There was one thing Michelangelo knew: without Granacci, there might be no Michelangelo.

In life, in relationships, through the good times and the difficult ones, as we take steps forward and grow, as we face setbacks, we get by with a little help from our friends.

Without our personal network, we simply lack the support we need to carry on in the face of obstacles. With support, the impossible seems possible.

Without support, we strain against the heavy weight. With support, the strength of two lifts the heavy weight with ease.

Without support, the Voice and its chiding are our only companions. With support, friendly words of encouragement lighten our path during the darkest part of the journey.

Without Granacci, no Michelangelo.

Jack

Let's go back to Jack, the marketing executive turned environmental activist from Chapter 3. Everything was looking good for Jack. His vision was clear, and he had a plan. He was ready to go and make a breakthrough in his career. He was raring to get his hands dirty working for an environmental preservation organization.

And so Jack began his job search. He scoured the Internet for opportunities. He refreshed his résumé and attached the press coverage of his Silver Forest triumph. When he read of an opening, he immediately followed up.

The résumés wended their way to directors of organizations, who would open and read Jack's materials with enthusiasm, impressed with Jack's skills and conviction and, frankly, curious about this marketing executive who wanted to save the earth.

After a few weeks Jack's phone would ring. He had landed an interview.

At the interview, Jack's knowledge and charm wove a strong presentation. The interviewer was compelled by his story, his passion for the environment, his experience in marketing and communications. When the conversation ended with a firm handshake and a smile, the director would say, "Good luck." And Jack would never hear back from the director.

Over and over again the same scenario played out.

Despite his conviction, professionalism, and clarity of vision, Jack alone couldn't get anyone to take him seriously. Just think how hard it would be for someone to convince the director of an environmental institution that a marketing executive who specialized in chemicals and pharmaceutical accounting products was right for the job.

When Jack and I spoke about his search, he wore his frustrations on his sleeve. "I'm at a loss. Everyone says I'm a great fit for this sort of work. But they won't hire me. One person even told me that I'm a work in progress who's already progressed beyond the professional level of most works that are finished. I'm not even sure what that means! But I think it means I have to go back to searching for work in marketing."

>>> *Use your personal network.* <<<

"Maybe you just need to think of other possibilities for expanding your search?" I offered. "You've been trying to do this all on your own. Maybe you should try to connect to work through your personal network. With the support and recommendation of someone who knows someone, you're more than just an anonymous job seeker."

For the next hour, Jack and I brainstormed ideas for connections. We mapped all the people in his personal network on a large sheet of paper. The husband of a former colleague who was an environmental lawyer with the state government. The owner of the organic food market, who published a popular environmental blog in his spare time. The people whom Jack had worked with in fighting for Silver Forest.

The people from Silver Forest! Somehow, in his plan, Jack had forgotten to involve his most loyal allies in his job search. If he could put the word out to his partners in that endeavor, perhaps they could connect him to others in the environmental world and give Jack the credibility he desired. Without them, Jack couldn't have saved Silver Forest. Now without them, he couldn't save himself.

Jack ran down the list of everyone he had ever known who had worked in environmental preservation or who simply took an interest in recycling. When Jack got to the Rs in his PalmPilot, he reached Rita Ronson—one of the women most involved in helping to fight the development.

After a few minutes of conversation with Rita, he discovered that she knew the director of a land trust who might be looking to hire someone. The next day, with Rita's referral, Jack found himself scheduling an interview with the trust's founder and executive director.

-»» *Expect the unexpected.* «-

That night, Jack's hands grasped his pillow, his body tossing it to and fro, trying not to wake his wife. Inside, Jack spun possible interview conversations in his head, over and over. When his alarm rang at 7 A.M., Jack might not have slept well, but he was prepared for his interview.

It was not at all what he expected.

When Jack arrived at the interview location, he knew he wasn't in corporate America anymore. The executive director's office was in an 1830s farmhouse constructed of stone, mortar, and oak from the wilds of nineteenth-century New Jersey.

Inside, the executive director sat at a wooden farm table surrounded by stacks of paper, antiques, and a wall of maps. She herself was an oddity. Hair askew, amber beads around her neck, overalls, construction boots—every inch of her was far from the suited executives with whom Jack had spent the majority of his career. In fact, this executive director made every other not-for-profit administrator seem as tailored as a Fortune 100 CEO.

Jack squinted as he entered, his eyes Photoshopping the gray from her hair. This is exactly what she must have looked like when she founded the organization in 1969. "Pull up a chair," she said in a voice that was gruff, friendly, and playful all at once. "Lots to do, lots to do."

Jack took a rickety chair as Hannah, the executive director, took off on a wild ride of a monologue. How she heard of his work through Rita. How she was impressed with his skills, but that didn't matter because anyone could learn this job. How he had passion for the land, and that mattered. How she needed someone with his skills in communications right away. How she couldn't pay him much. And then it was, "What the hell, you want to work for me?"

Jack's head was blown back. This woman was a cyclone, and Jack was swept up in her wake. "Why the hell not!" Jack blurted out.

That night Jack slept for a solid ten hours. He would have slept longer if it weren't for his daughter rushing into his room and jumping on the bed. "Congratulations, Daddy! You got a job!"

"Yes I did, honey. I did." He tossed his daughter into the air. All indications pointed to a beautiful morning.

Jack's career in the corporate world had taught him to expect a few things. With his experience came rewards, financial rewards. At the end of his corporate career, Jack had been making well over six figures. Considering how his skills in marketing had resulted in millions of dollars in corporate revenue, he was worth every penny.

The not-for-profit world, however, was a different world.

⋙ *Gain requires sacrifice.* ⋘

That day, when Jack received the offer from the land trust—if you consider a phone call in which the caller states "if you can start tomorrow, we'll pay you $40,000 a year" an offer—the difference between the corporate world and the not-for-profit world of environmental preservation became palpably clear.

Jack paused. This was the start of his masterpiece. How could he say no? At the same time, this was only a third of his previous salary; with his protracted job search eating up his severance pay and his savings, with his wife working part-time for little money and spending most of the time caring for their family, with the lifestyle he was accustomed to, how could he say yes?

Jack asked for forty-eight hours to sleep on the offer. But let's just say, that night Jack wasn't sleeping.

The next day I myself awoke to a message from Jack. The message was time-stamped 4 A.M. "So, I've got an offer. The job is exactly what I want. But there's no possible way I could ever take it. I've crunched the numbers. They're only offering me $40,000. And you know what I'm used to making, and well, um . . . Can we talk tomorrow? I mean today. Uh. Later."

When I called back first thing that morning, I reached a worried man. Jack was facing the true test of his conviction. In the abstract, of course, his dream seemed appealing, but here in front of him it was, well, real and therefore full of imperfections.

True, Jack and I had both recognized that he would have to take a cut in salary to achieve his vision, but this was a greater cut than either of us had imagined, and worse, it was the only offer at the end of a long road of frustrating interviews. If Jack was going to keep moving forward, if he was going to fulfill his vision and create his masterpiece, he would need the strength to take the risk, overcome the obstacle, and survive.

> ⇒⇒ *Get help from your closest supporters*
> *to confront your biggest fears.* ⇐⇐

"Let's for a second play a little game," I said to Jack. "Now imagine you've taken this job. It's Friday. Payday. Picture yourself collecting your paycheck from the boss. And now open the envelope."

"OK. I'm opening the envelope."

"Now look at the check. The small check. Take it in. Right now, looking at it, what's your biggest fear?"

"I can't support my family!"

"You don't think you could support your family?"

"Not in the way I am accustomed to."

"What would you miss the most?"

"Our vacations to St. Thomas. I mean, the whole family would miss that. We all work so hard. Sometimes you just need to get away from all the stress."

"But if you love the work you're doing . . ."

"Well, I guess you don't really need to go away to paradise if you're living your dreams."

"And what about a few days at the Jersey Shore? It's not as exotic, but it can be even more relaxing without the long-distance travel."

"OK. But what about my wife? She's been working at a not-for-profit for a while now."

"And you supported her in that decision?"

"Yes."

"Don't you think she'll support your decision?"

"She does."

"Together, how could you find a way to respond to your fears about financially supporting your family?"

That night, Jack tried to get to sleep as his wife, Sarah, sat up reading under the nightstand light. Again he tossed and turned. No luck. "Try counting sheep," he thought, "that always works in the cartoons."

There they were in Jack's busy mind: happy, fluffy, peaceful sheep. They frolicked over the fence. One, two, three. Then all of a sudden, from out of nowhere, flew an industrial-sized beard trimmer. The trimmer was buzzing with all Jack's fears about his job offer. And it was heading right for the peaceful, happy, fluffy, white sheep.

Soon, they were all totally bald.

"Bald!" shouted Jack, his eyes popping open and looking right into his wife's blue eyes.

"Having trouble sleeping?" Sarah asked. "Come on." She put her book down and pulled Jack out of bed.

Downstairs, Jack and Sarah talked about everything that had been bothering him the past few days. An hour later, they were in their home office, planning a budget for their family based on Jack making a salary of $40,000 a year.

Jack and Sarah bounced ideas off each other. They could each pack a lunch of leftovers and save on the $7 sandwich. Family vacations could be taken at Jack's family home down at the shore. There would be no new Volvo for Jack at the end of the year. And if the first or the fifteenth rolled around and it didn't look as if they would make a payment, there was always their savings to dip into, provided they were careful and didn't dig too deep. Whatever they did, they promised to work together and make sure that their family was secure while both of them were following their dreams.

As the sun came up, Jack and Sarah were still poring over spreadsheets. It was Jack's second night without sleep. Strangely, he felt invigorated.

Jack pulled his eyes from the spreadsheet and took in Sarah. There she was, looking at their life together in dollars and cents. The way her brow wrinkled as she thought, how her lips moved as she did calculations in her head, these were the most precious things he had ever seen. No matter how much Jack cut back on cars, vacations, lunches, or anything else, he would still always have Sarah's priceless love. And no matter what happened in his life, Sarah would be there to help him through.

Sarah caught Jack looking at her. "Is something wrong?"

Jack could only respond with a kiss. What words could ever communicate this feeling?

He laid his hand gently on his wife's heart.

Without Sarah, no Jack.

The Medici Connection

Without his friend Francesco Granacci's intervention, Michelangelo might never have embarked upon a career in the arts. But how far would he have gotten as an artist without additional support? Greatness requires a certain degree of freedom—financial freedom and freedom to experiment—and such freedom was not generally available to young artists. During the Renaissance, art was produced in *fabbricas* (factories); most artists were viewed like today's blue-collar workers. Michelangelo's family, being wool merchants, considered his choice to work in Ghirlandaio's *fabbrica* to be beneath them.

>>> *Greatness requires freedom.* <<<

There were a few renowned painters who controlled the *fabbricas*. They trained youngsters as apprentices, primarily to fill in "cartoons" or base drawings that the master created. If the hirelings showed talent, they were given the opportunity later on to help in more creative aspects of the process.

The masters made sure that they retained all the credit themselves for any great work. Actually, though, the art attributed to a great master was often executed by a number of his workers, all of whom remained anonymous.

This is the way the master wanted it. Fame was not to be shared. Unlike today's movies, there was no list of credits telling who was part of the team—no telling who was "best boy." So there is no way of even knowing which of Ghirlandaio's paintings were worked on by Michelangelo.

As we have seen, Michelangelo separated himself from the crowd of other apprentices through a bit of arrogance and a dash of risk taking. He took a drawing by his master Ghirlandaio and improved upon it. People talked, word got out. The boy could draw!

⫸ *Fame is short-lived without enduring support.* ⫷

But this sort of fame tends to be short-lived unless you can gain long-lasting support that will take you to the next level. Michelangelo found this support in no less a personage than Lorenzo de' Medici—Florence's political leader, head of the city-state's most powerful family, and known to all as Lorenzo the Magnificent.

It may seem odd to us today that a political leader would be the one to nurture artistic genius. But in the Renaissance, it was not only the artists like Michelangelo and Leonardo who had a wide breadth of interests and talents. The great rulers during the period also strove to be "Renaissance men"—and none more so than Lorenzo the Magnificent, whose interests and accomplishments spanned the worlds of politics, banking, and the arts.

As luck would have it, shortly after Michelangelo corrected his master's drawing, Lorenzo was seeking to start a school for sculpture, an art that was largely lacking in Florence. Michelangelo made sure that his name was considered and, once in the school, did what he needed to do to distinguish himself.

Lorenzo recognized Michelangelo's talent and supported it. He even brought Michelangelo to live in his household. There, in close contact with the best and the brightest of Florence, Michelangelo received an invaluable informal education—absorbing philosophy, poetry, art, and the classics and developing his independent spirit.

From this great family, Michelangelo later obtained the commissions necessary for financial independence. Among his commissions were the great Medici tombs, the Medici family church of San Lorenzo, and the Laurentian Library for the rare collection of books owned by the Medici family.

Saving Michelangelo's Life

Michelangelo's connection to the family is likely to have saved his life after the fall of the Republic of Florence in 1529 when Bartolommeo Valori, the new commissioner, ordered his murder. Alessandro Corsini, a member of Florence's Council of Two Hundred, was determined to assassinate Michelangelo to avenge Michelangelo's support for the republic and a long-standing family grudge against Michelangelo for having dissected the corpse of a young Corsini relative many years earlier. Michelangelo, having heard about the warrant for his death, hid in the house of a friend until a pardon could be arranged from Clement VII (a Medici pope). Clement, who was concerned about Michelangelo's failing health, reinstated Michelangelo's allowance and ordered him to work only on the Medici tombs.

Nurture, support, protection—Michelangelo needed it all and found it during one of the most turbulent periods in history. We, too, need nurture, support, and protection in our own turbulent lives.

Barbara

"Semper Fi" is the Marine Corps motto, short for the Latin *semper fidelis* (always faithful). Faithful to God, country, family, and the Corps. Barbara, a strikingly attractive and fit woman now in her early forties, has a Semper Fi decal on her car. In true Marine tradition, whenever another Marine, active or retired, sees the decal, a salute and an enthusiastic and crisp "Semper Fi" greeting is exchanged.

Barbara joined the Corps right after graduation from high school, partly to escape an alcoholic and overbearing father, partly to make her parents proud, but mostly because her longtime best friend, Mary Ann, wanted to go. Mary Ann was the daring one. Barbara called her "the Unsinkable Molly Brown" because she seemed unafraid of anything and was an eternal optimist. Mary Ann was the perfect counterbalance to Barbara's fearful, overprotective mother. Rather than giving all the reasons why Barbara couldn't or shouldn't do something, Mary Ann provided reasons why she might want to try something new. Barbara began to see life as full of possibilities and opportunities, not dangers and problems.

Barbara was elated that Mary Ann would be stationed at the same base after graduation from boot camp—assignments were made alphabetically, and their last names started with the same letter. At their new station more than a thousand miles from home, something unpredictable started to happen. As Barbara told it, "I always thought of Mary Ann as the strong one, but being away from her close family life was harder for her than for me. She cried every Sunday. She didn't want to be there. So I helped her more than she helped me to adjust to our new life." Barbara continued, "At one point Mary Ann said, 'I don't want to be better than you—I want to be just like you.' And that was just what I was thinking about her."

Barbara and Mary Ann made new friends in the Marine Corps. They learned about being in a "band of brothers and sisters" and what *esprit de corps* really means—a common spirit of comradeship, enthusiasm, and devotion to a cause among the members of a group. Nurture (in the Marines that sometimes means "tough love"), support, and protection were the standing orders of the day. And that support helped both Barbara and her best friend grow in directions they never imagined.

Upon returning home from the Corps, Barbara earned her college degree compliments of Uncle Sam. In college she met and married Kevin, a man fifteen years her senior, who had been sent by his management consulting firm to earn an M.B.A. degree. After graduation, Barbara worked at a fitness and nutrition center, and a few years later she and Kevin moved to the suburbs, where their son, Peter, was born. Barbara had expected to be a full-time mom until Peter started school. But Kevin, who had a high-stress job and had ignored Barbara's pleas to exercise and watch his diet, had a stroke and then a fatal heart attack.

Barbara was left with a very nice house and a beautiful son but little else. Kevin hadn't believed in life insurance. "We can do better investing the money ourselves," he had said. But in fact they had put all their money into buying their home, so no money remained to invest.

Barbara was now a single mom in a strange community with a young child and no means of financial support. She got a job as an office temp, which she hated. "But what else could I do?" she asked me when we met for the first time. She felt trapped, trying to cope at home and struggling on her low income.

Barbara came to me to talk about finding a different kind of work, but mostly she talked about her loneliness. She told me about her friendship with Mary Ann, who now lived two states away and had three kids. Because of this, contact was limited. Barbara's new neighbors were friendly but a bit standoffish, and she couldn't understand why.

"Have you reached out to them?" I asked.

"I had a barbecue and invited the entire neighborhood. A lot of people came and seemed to have a good time. They called to thank me, but then nothing. . . ." Her voice faded to a whisper of disappointment.

"What did you talk about at the barbecue?" I asked.

"We talked about our kids and how they're doing, of course. Mostly, though, they were curious about my experience in the Marines. What it was like to be a woman in the Corps."

"What did you say?" I asked.

"I talked mostly about the inner strength that you need to survive the experience. And how good you felt when you did survive. How you felt that now you could face anything on your own. No matter how difficult."

"Maybe your neighbors feel that you don't need them. You more or less told them that yourself."

"But this is different. They must see that," Barbara responded.

"I'm not sure that they do. Why don't you reach out to one of them, have lunch, and open up with her?" I suggested.

⇛ *When you are drowning and someone throws you a life preserver, grab it.* ⇜

Barbara invited her neighbor Cindy for lunch. Over chicken salad and lemon cake, they each spoke of their lives—their dreams, their disappointments, their hopes for their children. Cindy met the real Barbara. The following Saturday, Cindy invited Barbara to a local art gallery and lunch with four other neighbors.

Once they got to really know Barbara, these women quickly became her "band of sisters." "They were a lifeline for me, and I appreciated it," Barbara said. "When you are drowning and someone throws you a life preserver, you'd better grab on to it!"

As the months passed, Barbara found with this group of women the companionship and emotional support she needed. This "band of sisters" exhibited the same esprit de corps she had experienced in the Marine Corps—comradeship, enthusiasm, and devotion to each other.

Barbara and I continued to meet about her job situation. We began with assessments and exercises to get at her values. Faith in God, adventure, friendship, family, nutrition, and fitness were high on her list. Self-respect was at the top.

Through dialogue and assessments, we uncovered her passion and strengths. Barbara loved vegetarian cooking, particularly creating new recipes for delicious, healthy meals. Over the next few months, she frequently brought a special dish she made to get-togethers with her new friends. Her primary strengths turned out to be her exceptional listening skills and her capacity to empathize with others.

We were ready to begin a series of sessions to uncover career possibilities. I suggested that Barbara might want to talk to her friends and see if together they could come up with career ideas that related to her values, passions, and strengths.

Barbara arrived at our next session very excited. She had been talking to Cindy, who told her that the town's health food store, the Healthy Way, was up for sale. One thing had led to another, and they ended up discussing becoming partners and buying the store.

"I just don't know," Barbara said. "I'd really, really love to do it, but I don't have any money to invest."

We spent a very constructive session figuring out how to make it work. If Cindy could come up with the down payment, they might be able to borrow the rest. And Barbara would be willing to do the lion's share of the work if she could take a small salary. Barbara could then quit her job as an office temp. "That would be incredible!" she said, her eyes sparkling.

Three months later, Barbara and Cindy bought the store and renamed it Wholesome Harvest. Cindy came up with the cash, and the local savings and loan company provided the rest.

I had a feeling the store would be a success the first time I went for a visit. Barbara was busy chatting away with the customers, making them feel at home and patiently answering their questions. "Is there a natural remedy for arthritic pain?" one customer asked. Barbara suggested she try arnica. "Is there anything that can help with my headaches?" another inquired. Barbara recommended chamomile tea and brought out some products with special herbs. "What do you recommend for acid reflux?" someone else requested. Barbara responded with recipes that were low in acid.

Barbara nurtured everyone who came into the store—not only through providing healthy food for the body, but through enlivening conversation for the soul. She considered this her "personal ministry." She showed real concern for her customers' needs. They, in turn, made the store a success, buying the natural and organic products she provided.

After two years it was clear the store needed to be fixed up and expanded. Some additional money was required, which could have come from reinvesting the profits. But Barbara suggested that it would be fun to involve the rest of the "band of sisters," who became enthusiastic partners.

I saw Barbara weekly at her health food store. She had stopped being my client a long time ago, but I continued to be her customer. I looked forward to our interesting discussions about food and community issues and often ended up buying more organic vegetables than I could use for the week.

⇒⟫ *Review your goals and progress from time to time.* ⟪⇐

On one of my visits, Barbara asked if she could meet with me at my office. We set up an appointment for later that week. I was very curious about what Barbara's problem might be.

"I turned forty years old last month, and it made me start to consider where I've been and where I'm going. I loved my mother and appreciate all she gave me. But I think she lived a small life, and I never wanted my children to say that about me. I want to live a life that makes me proud and will make my friends and son proud of me. I thought a meeting with you might be useful to give me some direction."

I pointed out that many people use the "big birthdays" as touchstones to consider their lives. "For many people, thirty means the end of youth and forty the beginning of middle age," I said. "Considering your goals and progress is a very healthy thing to do from time to time."

I kept probing during our meeting for what might be missing in her life. She seemed to have it all: meaningful work, wonderful friends, a loving son, and a healthy lifestyle.

I asked her to write down her goals for the next three months, why she wanted them, and what benefits the achievement of each goal would bring to others. There on the page was revealed the blueprint for her extraordinary life: Continue to help others through her "personal ministry" at the health food store; continue the journey she had begun with the "band of sisters"; and continue to love, nurture, and support her son.

As Barbara studied this list, I could see her smile broaden. Then as the revelation took hold and the meaning become clear, her eyes welled up and tears began to fall gently. She realized that she was already leading the extraordinary life of which she, her son, and her friends could be proud.

Sculpt Your Personal Masterpiece

Without Francesco Granacci, who provided the young Michelangelo with emotional and artistic support and helped secure for him an apprenticeship with Domenico Ghirlandaio, the foremost painter in Florence, there might have been no Michelangelo. Without a little help from our friends, creating a masterpiece is a lonely and difficult endeavor. But find your support, and the arduous path to your extraordinary life becomes easier to navigate.

Before you find your support, however, you need to determine what type of support you need. Support comes in many forms, such as guidance, information, money, and personal connections. Find the right support, and your breakthrough will come more easily.

Your support network could include people whose emotional support you need, like family and friends. It could involve those whose lives might be dramatically affected by the changes you seek to make. Or it could consist of those whose assistance you need to achieve your goals.

As you look for support, be wary of naysayers and those who drain your energy. Like the Voice, these people will do everything to diminish your drive even though they may mean well. Instead, surround yourself with people who support your personal values, who understand your passions, and who believe in your vision.

To find your support, it's important to be vocal about your vision and your plans to achieve it. Let everyone know of your commitment to your vision. Inspire them with your confidence. Work hard to demonstrate the success of your plan.

Before you actively seek someone's help, think about these questions:

+ Are they sufficiently committed to my efforts, and will they follow through as promised?

+ What do I expect from them?

+ What are they expecting from me?

+ Are my expectations of this person or organization realistic?

+ What is this person truly feeling about my request for help?

Discovery Exercises

1. Take out your personal address book, PalmPilot, or Rolodex. Select as many people or organizations as you can find (ten to fifty) that might be helpful to you. Prepare a list of the names and contact information, including the areas in which they might support you in achieving your goals.

2. Take a look at the list. Prioritize it based on who you think will be most likely to help. Rewrite the list with your most likely support at the top.

3. Now go down the list and contact each person or organization. Share with them your preliminary ideas about your vision of an extraordinary life. Ask them for ideas on how you might pursue that vision. Ask them to connect you to people in their personal network who might be able to help.

4. Find a professional organization that relates to your career or life choice. Attend one of its meetings or a conference or workshop that it has organized. Make as many contacts as you can. Follow up with these new contacts to get additional information about the career or life choice you are considering. Congratulate yourself for getting the ball rolling!

Ceiling of the Sistine Chapel

Although he always considered himself a sculptor, Michel-angelo is perhaps best known today for his unsurpassed physical and creative achievement of painting more than three hundred figures in fresco over a four-year period covering the 132-by-44-foot ceiling of the Sistine Chapel at the Vatican in Rome. These figures were grouped into three major themes: the creation of the world, the creation of man, and the fall and punishment of man.

Photography courtesy of Art Resource

7

. . . .

Fight for Your Vision

The Pope was relentlessly urging Michelangelo to finish the ceiling of the Sistine Chapel. On one occasion, among others, Michelangelo replied, "It will be finished when I shall have satisfied myself in the matter of art."

—Life of Michelangelo,
Giorgio Vasari, 1568

Pope Julius II was anxious to show to the world Michelangelo's great fresco on the ceiling of the Sistine Chapel. He himself had not been able to view it properly. When he climbed the scaffold to see it up close, he could see it only piecemeal and would lose the proper perspective that distance provided. And when seen from the ground, the mas sive scaffolding completely obscured the work. The pope "was by nature impetuous and impatient of waiting" (Ascanio Condivi, 1553) and raged at Michelangelo's slow progress in completing the work.

When the ceiling still had some unfinished sections and required a final coat of paint, Pope Julius ordered that the scaffolding be torn down. But the ceiling had not yet reached the full form of Michelangelo's vision. And if Michelangelo were to honor the pope's wishes, and if he were to pull the scaffolding down, Michelangelo could never bring the work to completion. After all, the scaffolding would take months to rebuild, and once the impatient pope saw the frescoes, even if incomplete, he would never want them covered again.

Still, this was, after all, the pope of the Holy Roman Church. And the voice of God on earth insisted he take down the scaffolding.

Michelangelo had a choice: stand his ground, deny the pope's wishes, climb the scaffolding, and continue his hard work or heed the pope's words, tear down the scaffolding, and leave his masterpiece forever unfinished. Fight his church or run out on his vision.

Michelangelo chose to fight.

When Michelangelo refused to take the scaffolding down, the pope struck him with his staff and ordered the workers to remove the scaffolding despite what Michelangelo said. Michelangelo, enraged, gathered himself and stormed out of the chapel and headed home, shouting that he was going back to Florence and never returning to Rome.

As Michelangelo scurried around his home packing his things for the trip to Florence, a knock came at his door. It was the pope's emissaries. The pope, seeing Michelangelo's conviction, experienced a change of heart. And now he begged Michelangelo to return to his work and finish it in his own fashion.

Michelangelo was vindicated. He had fought for his vision, and he had won.

The truth is, creating a masterpiece is messy. It involves splashes of paint on the floor, flying particles of marble, accidents that destroy compositions, struggles to understand your own direction, various obstacles to completing your work—procrastination, lack of funds, depression, and illness. Many great artists die penniless and alone. Many masterpieces hide half-finished in attics. Others are imperfect, marred by compromise.

You see, when nothing seems to go your way, you have two choices: you can decide that it's just not meant to be and run out on your dream, or you can stand your ground and fight for your vision.

But in truth, there's hardly a choice to make—that is, if you want to realize the masterpiece you're meant to create. When the choice is between fight or flight, choose to stay and fight.

Catherine

Catherine always rooted for the underdog. She loved her hapless New York Mets. She took in stray dogs and sick cats. Catherine's business, as you will recall, was even about the underdogs of the American economy—the small businesses to whom she provided administrative and technical services.

But Catherine herself wasn't an underdog when she started her business. In fact, if you looked closely at the market, Catherine had the advantage.

At the time, many talented people, like Catherine, were downsized out of their jobs and, rather than work for someone else, decided to start something for themselves. Coming from a company that had laid off hundreds of smart, productive workers, Catherine had access to a ready client base.

Catherine understood this opportunity, and she worked it to her advantage. She hardly even needed to pick up a phone. Once the people in her personal network discovered what she could do for their small business, Catherine was flooded with leads. It looked like Catherine was going to succeed solely on the basis of her personal contacts. She couldn't believe it was so easy.

⋙ Success requires discipline. ⋘

As a young woman, Catherine had been remarkably fit. Having trained and performed as an opera singer, she had to keep herself in shape. For while the stereotype of the opera singer is the hefty diva in the horned helmet, the reality is that opera singers are athletes; their body is their instrument. Catherine was no exception; she kept her body in extraordinary condition.

That was then. As Catherine moved away from her work in opera and entered the corporate world, her athletic discipline slowly turned soft. When she reached her late forties, she found herself very overweight.

Something had to change. And so, at her previous job, Catherine had made a radical change in her life. She committed to eating healthier foods and exercising, which had resulted in a dramatic weight loss of more than forty pounds.

Every time Catherine stepped in front of the mirror, she couldn't help smiling. She was proud of her ability to change the things she didn't like about herself.

But when Catherine started her own business, that image in the mirror had begun to grow larger. With the rush of initial clients and the effort of setting up her own business, Catherine found herself working harder than ever. The work took a toll on the quality of her life.

With the stress of her increased workload, Catherine found it harder and harder to keep up with her healthy eating habits. She simply had no time to shop for vegetables or grill salmon. She did, however, have time for the McDonald's drive-through. It is called fast food for a reason, and Catherine was eating more and more of it.

It wasn't just her diet. Catherine found herself eating between visits with clients. She ate constantly while sitting in front of her computer. All that she had learned about healthy living had flown out the window.

In a few months, the weight Catherine had lost returned. Her energy dwindled. She found it harder to climb stairs. On days when she worked out of her home, she sometimes took a midday nap, just to keep going.

Something didn't seem right. Sure, she had stopped eating well, but even when she was at her heaviest, she wasn't having these problems.

>> *Your priorities must change*
to meet your current reality. <<

Catherine nervously sat in the waiting room. She began to ponder the list of things that could possibly be wrong with her.

The doctor was ready to see her.

When Catherine described her symptoms to the doctor, he couldn't hide his concern. He ordered tests. After the blood work came back, he ordered a mammogram. A week later, as the doctor showed her the film, it was clear. Catherine had a growth in her left breast. The doctor suspected it was cancerous. A biopsy confirmed his suspicions. Catherine had cancer. She would need surgery and chemotherapy if she was going to survive.

Catherine couldn't speak. She nodded at the doctor, trying to grasp what he was telling her. For the next six months, her life would change radically. During the course of cancer treatment, there was no way she was going to be able to function as she had. Her business was now the least of her worries.

After the surgeon removed the tumor from her left breast, Catherine underwent chemotherapy. For five months, Catherine made the hard trek back and forth to the hospital for the treatments. For the first few days of each course of treatment, she suffered through debilitating nausea and weakness. A few days would pass, and Catherine would slowly recover. And then, just as she was feeling somewhat better, she would go through it all again.

Catherine lost her hair. She struggled daily to sit up in bed. She lost weight at a rapid clip. But at the end of the five months, she was back in her doctor's office with the cancer in complete remission.

Catherine felt energized. Life had a clarity and purpose now that she had come close to the edge. Every day was precious. It was time to get back to her vision.

⇛ *Fight your way through life's ebbs and flows.* ⇚

Life doesn't simply do whatever we want it to do. There's an ebb and flow. Sometimes things go smoothly. Your new business shows success out of the gate. You change your lifestyle, eat healthier, and lose forty pounds. You look incredible on the red carpet as you go to accept your Oscar. But sometimes life hands you cancer. It's up to us to recognize the flow, anticipate the ebb, and fight to move through it.

When Catherine finally returned to her business after six months, there was more ebb than flow. It got so bad at one point that she began to worry if she would ever have customers again. She waited by the phone, hoping it would ring, hoping some of her previous clients would make the referrals that drove her early success. Finally, after a month of no business, she called me to set up a coaching appointment.

"I don't understand what's happened. Everything was going so well a year ago. Maybe I didn't do a good job," Catherine lamented when we met.

The Voice had clearly come back into Catherine's life. "Do you really think it's that you didn't do a good job or that you were terribly ill?" I asked.

"I know, I know. I'm letting the Voice get the best of me. But I just can't understand it. Here I was, my business surging with clients, and now, six months later, the tap is completely dry. With all I've been through, I just don't have the cash flow to last through these low tides."

"Do you have to simply last? You have a vision. What's getting in the way of that vision?"

"My ability to get clients."

"What's getting in the way of finding clients?"

Catherine avoided my gaze. Frankly, she was just avoiding something, though I wasn't sure what that was. "OK. I know. I need to start a marketing program. I know how to do it. I guess I'll just have to do it."

"What's the worst thing that could happen if you played full-out on a marketing program?"

"I guess that I wouldn't get any new clients."

"Well, that sounds like where you are now."

Catherine sighed.

"And what's the best thing that could happen?"

"I'd be able to grow my business, bring on extra employees, and retire in Italy and while away my days listening to Puccini."

"The question you need to ask yourself is whether you are willing to fight to achieve the success you want. The difference between success and failure isn't how strong your vision is—it's how hard you're willing to fight for it." We talked through her issues and blocks and made a plan.

The next morning, Catherine started to implement the plan. She began to show how hard she was willing to fight. She assembled a list of possible contacts. She reached out to former clients for referrals. She mapped out a plan to achieve her revenue goals. She prepared a list of potential clients to call on. In less than two weeks, Catherine was ready to take action.

>>> *Fight through your insecurities to avoid procrastination.* <<<

Catherine hated cold-calling. She sat at her table, the telephone before her. Catherine pulled her call sheet from the folder and contemplated where to start. The obvious place would be the As, of course, but then again, she could start from the middle—or the end. She could even jump around: C to A to X or Y.

Catherine traced columns to make sure she got the salient information for her database. She put on Wagner to psych herself up. She was ready. But oh, wait! She would need a fresh glass of water. Must keep those vocal cords hydrated. Then she needed to feed her cat. A hungry Whiskers would surely interrupt her while she was closing a deal.

By the time Catherine was ready to make the first call, two hours had passed. Finally, she picked up the phone. Ten voice mail messages later, she reached her first prospect.

"Hello," said the resonant basso of the stranger. Catherine's finger held his name on her call sheet: Mr. Jerry Tzechekski.

Tzechekski?! Catherine's heart pounded like a Brazilian dance hall. She attempted to pronounce the name in her mind. She could never pronounce the name Tzechekski! But she better say something fast.

"Hi Jerry, this is Catherine O'Connell with SBC Associates." Her voice cracked. Here she was, a former professional opera singer, and her voice cracked! This was not going well. "I was hoping to take a moment of your time to . . ." Catherine stopped for a moment of contemplation; she began to feel that this might be a bad time for this Jerry. Yes, this was a bad time. "I'm sorry, am I reaching you at a good time?"

"Actually, I'm about to run to a meeting. Can you call back some other time?"

"Sure. OK. Thank you." She hung up, both frustrated and relieved.

And then the Voice returned. "Hey, Cath, if you can't pitch Jerry What's-it, what good are you?"

Catherine shook it off and looked to the call sheet. How can I get clients? And if I don't get clients, how can I pay my bills?

The call sheet had no answer.

When Catherine and I met the next week, she started right in with her litany of frustrations. "First, it was the glass ceiling, then the layoff, then cancer, now no clients and my own incompetence at selling. How will I ever get past all these obstacles?"

"Do you remember when you lost your job? When I asked you what the best thing was that could happen after losing your job, you said you could start your own business. Why did you say that?"

Catherine knew why. "Because I was tired of corporate executives judging what I could and couldn't do. And I wanted to make a difference in other people's lives by providing support services that would help them find more time and be more productive in their business."

"And I know you're passionate about doing that. And you're clearly trying to achieve your goals. You just have to be willing to have setbacks in order to succeed. Did you know the average small business owner has three unsuccessful businesses before he or she finds the right formula for success? The ones that do succeed fought for their vision every step of the way."

Catherine nodded her head quietly. "Yes, I know. I believe I'm a fighter. But how do I fight this?"

⇛ *Be innovative in fighting for your vision.* ⇚

If Catherine's business was going to survive despite all the challenges, she was going to have to fight for her vision in a different way.

Catherine knew what she was up against—her resistance to cold-calling and her tendency to get down on herself when things went wrong.

She also knew what her strengths were. Once Catherine had worked for someone, they willingly provided referrals. Catherine had an infectious passion and a confident, professional manner. And, most important, she was very good at what she did. If only the leads could seek her out and see what she could do, they would want to work with her.

What we needed was an innovative strategy to fight this battle. Catherine and I explored her options for doing things another way. How could she find clients without cold-calling? How could she show potential clients who she was without resorting to the formality of a grunt sales effort? We pondered the battlefield. If Catherine could only somehow have the people come to her so they could see her professionalism, passion, and high level of competence, they would want to work with her.

"What about networking?" I suggested. She immediately grabbed the thought and ran with it. If she could join a group of properly placed professionals, with face-to-face contact on a regular basis, she could convince them to begin sending potential clients her way. I mentioned several business network organizations that I knew of, and she decided to see if they had local chapters. A plan had hatched.

Within a week, Catherine had joined one of the network groups meeting in her area. The results were astounding. The woman who couldn't make a telephone call to a stranger had no problem exchanging business leads with people she met for a breakfast meeting once a week. Catherine industriously followed up on each lead she was given and was generous in helping other members of the group find clients. Catherine paved the way by making advance phone calls for group members, and they reciprocated for her. New friendships formed, and these led to additional contacts. Whenever possible she arranged to meet face-to-face with potential clients. After a few months her business again began to prosper.

Catherine, the survivor, had fought the most important battle in realizing her vision, and she had won.

Michelangelo and the Fortification of Florence

Choosing to fight the forces that oppose your vision is one thing. Choosing how to fight them is quite another. The fact is, if you fail to approach your battles in the right way, fighting will only lead to greater obstacles—and deeper failures.

Just imagine if you were actually fighting for your life and your homeland. Just imagine if what stood between you and your masterpiece was a foreign army. Imagine the fate of Michelangelo when, in April 1529, the Spanish and German armies sacked Rome and began the long march to Florence.

Michelangelo was a Florentine patriot. His *David* was chosen to stand in the public square of the city as a symbol of the protection of Florence and its way of life against all invaders. Michelangelo, of course, was also known to be one of the greatest creative geniuses of his generation. None of this was lost on Florence's ruling Council of Nine, which voted to put him in charge of designing the city's defenses. Michelangelo, who had never designed a fortification, took the challenge.

Traditionally, cities such as Florence were shielded from attack by their mountainous geography and by massive stone walls that marked the city's borders. This, in fact, was how Rome had been fortified. And Rome had just been sacked by the very army that was now marching on Florence. How could Michelangelo build a structure that would stop this seemingly unstoppable force?

Michelangelo thought about the coming onslaught. He anticipated the assault, marshaled his strength and resources, and developed a creative approach to protect his homeland.

After studying the terrain and style of warfare preferred by the attacking armies, Michelangelo recommended a radical approach to defending Florence. Rather than reinforcing the walls of the city, Michelangelo suggested they build a massive fortification on a hill that covered the main approach to Florence. From here not only could Florentines defend their city, they could also attack the foreign invaders.

But Michelangelo didn't stop there. He developed a number of crucial innovations. Unlike most fortifications at the time, Michelangelo's designs were not single towers. They were instead starlike structures with dips and slopes that permitted rapid deployment of reinforcements. In addition, Michelangelo's fortifications had artillery platforms that stood very high off the ground providing for greater range and making them less vulnerable to attack. Finally, Michelangelo created ingenious barriers to protect the tall campaniles, or bell towers, of the church and monastery, which were used as lookout points for offensive and defensive maneuvers.

In September 1529, Florence was attacked by a huge army of Spanish and German troops commanded by the Prince of Orange, reinforced by soldiers from Lombardy. Despite months of concerted effort, the foreign armies, harassed by attacking Florentine soldiers, were never able to breach Michelangelo's fortifications or to even destroy the campaniles.

⋙ *Anticipate the blows.* ⋘

Creating your masterpiece is a little like going to war. As you start the hard work of revealing your masterpiece to the world, that same world is coming at you, attacking your precious vision. You have no choice but to fight for what you believe in. Like Michelangelo did in his defense of Florence, you need to prepare for the blows, gather your energy and resources, and develop an innovative strategy.

Daniel

Daniel is the son of my best friend from college, Vince, so I know his story well. Daniel felt he could confide in me, and, from time to time, I would informally coach him. I asked him to come in to talk about his experiences and to allow me to share them with others to illustrate how, with determination, dreams can be deferred and recaptured.

Daniel loved baseball. He was good at it, too. A golden glove short-stop and the second best hitter on his high school team, he special-ized in line drive singles up the middle. With his ability to run like a gazelle, he led the team in stolen bases. Daniel's only weakness was his lack of power. At five feet, ten inches and weighing 150 pounds, he just didn't have the heft to hit the long ball. But he did have deter-mination. One day his coach said that he would give Daniel $100 if he hit a ball over the fence during a league game, a feat Daniel had never come close to accomplishing. Daniel worked out nearly every day in the weight room, building his strength, and sure enough, in the third to last game of the season, he won his $100.

Daniel knew exactly what he wanted to do when he became an adult—teach high school history and coach baseball. "I've loved baseball since I was three years old. And my father fostered my love of history. He loved to tell stories about how people lived years and years ago. I guess it made a deep impression on me. I think that people should pay more attention to the past."

Daniel's parents, Vince and Elizabeth, supported Daniel's passion for baseball, sending him to baseball camp in the summer, buying him the best equipment, and cheering at his games.

But their support and sacrifice extended well beyond sports. When Daniel was seven, they had moved to the suburbs so that he could enjoy the safety and fresh air of "the country." To do this, Vince commuted two hours each way to work, but he believed in sacrificing for his family.

For annual vacations Vince generally would plan a trip to one of the national parks, where they would view the spectacular landscapes and learn about natural history. En route, Elizabeth would teach her favorite rounds, which Vince and Daniel would sing— with mixed results. Daniel had his own Polaroid and loved capturing the landscape. Every evening he would paste the photos into his album and write a kind of journal of captions.

Holidays were also special. Thanksgiving brought at least a dozen relatives to their house. And on Christmas, no matter how cold, Elizabeth, Vince, and Daniel would go caroling through the neighborhood, sometimes joined by neighbors who would offer them hot drinks or come out and sing along.

Vince and Elizabeth believed in a loving, simple life—friends and family were very important; material goods much less so. They passed these values on to Daniel. They also passed on a strong work ethic. Vince had started as a bank teller and worked his way up to branch manager. Elizabeth worked first as a teacher's aide and then as a teacher in a day care center.

There was a good deal of structure at home, and Daniel had daily chores. He was responsible for keeping his room neat, washing the family's dishes, doing his own laundry, taking out the garbage, and walking the dog. Homework was from 7 to 9 P.M. each weekday. During the off-season for baseball, Daniel had a newspaper delivery route, and during the summer he worked at a baseball camp.

⟫ You can't always live the American dream. ⟪

Daniel and his family were living the American dream. Until, at age forty-three, Vince was diagnosed with a brain tumor. He had been wondering about a ringing in his ear for some time but had an aversion to doctors, so he never looked into it until the headaches started. Unfortunately, the cancer advanced quickly. Less than a year later, Vince was dead. He left his family free of debt but without much in the way of assets other than the proceeds from a small insurance policy.

"I didn't know Dad was dying until it happened," Daniel said. "I was shocked. I wasn't at the hospital much because I didn't know how bad it was, and that troubled me for a long time after. It was very difficult. There are a lot of things that a kid needs his father for. It was a struggle for the first few years, and it didn't get much better later."

Elizabeth struggled to maintain the lifestyle that she and Daniel had enjoyed before Vince died. She returned to work full time, and friends and family helped care for Daniel when she couldn't be there for him. She became deeply depressed with trying to do it all. "Everything, and I mean *everything*, scared my mother," Daniel remarked. Later on she was diagnosed with multiple sclerosis. "Her body was breaking down," Daniel said. "This disease also affects your brain. She was very irrational much of the time. At first I got really angry at her, and I would yell a lot because she was being so unreasonable. The social worker explained that it was the MS."

By the time Daniel was in high school, the money was running out. I tried to help Elizabeth cut her expenses and create a budget, but she was unable to cope with all the responsibilities, depression, and now MS. Daniel, age sixteen, stepped up to the plate again, this time to help his mother manage their budget.

"When I was a junior, I started working full time after school because we didn't have much money left. At the time, I was just working at the video store. I did a deal where I pretty much ran the whole store toward the end of my senior year in high school. The owner put me in charge of managing the money and all that stuff. I had to miss a lot of things that people my age do. I couldn't go out with my friends because I had to work late at the store."

Fate in the form of a big insurance check intervened. When he was fifteen, Daniel had gone flying on a small plane piloted by a friend's uncle. "We had to get over this row of trees but instead went right into it. It was my side of the plane that actually hit the tree. I was hurt pretty badly. They medevacked me to Morristown Hospital. It was tough recovering physically, but when the settlement came in years later, it did give me the money to buy the video store. At the time that I bought the store, what I really wanted to do was go to college. But it didn't work out. I had too many responsibilities at home."

Daniel, now age eighteen, was committed to making the store a success. "We really needed the money. I worked like crazy—all day, every day, seven days a week, thirteen hours a day. For one year I got up, went to the store, went home, and went to sleep. I didn't do anything else.

"While all of my friends went to college and their parents pretty much paid for them, I was struggling for everything I had. I basically had to take charge of my mother and manage things for her. I got her home mortgage refinanced under my name at a much lower rate and used the extra money to fix up the house. When I was twenty, I was like someone thirty-five trying to take care of a family."

> ⇒⟫ *Sometimes it's better to be lucky than good.* ⟪⇐

"I sold the video store before the business started to fade. I was really lucky. Eventually, competition from things like the big chains, movies on demand, and Internet rental services started to kill independent video stores. I got out just in time. Pure luck. It wasn't like I saw it coming. I just couldn't keep up what I was doing any longer."

Now at age twenty-one, Daniel had a modest nest egg. He decided he had to figure out a way to get his mother the help she needed and to get his own life on track. He spoke with some of his mother's friends and family to see if they could provide some help. Her brother agreed to have her live with him. Daniel visited her often but now was free to revisit his own dreams.

> ⇒⟫ *A dream deferred too long is often a dream lost.* ⟪⇐

Daniel could have used the money to spend the year taking it easy: traveling, relaxing at beaches, watching ball games on TV. He had certainly earned some time off. But Daniel realized that a dream deferred too long is often a dream lost. He was anxious to recapture his dream of teaching history and coaching baseball.

"I was accepted to college and am in school full time now—doing what I want to do for the first time in six years. My college experience isn't going to be like the ones my friends had. I'm older. It'll be just study and go. But if I had to miss out on a few things to help my mother out, that's what had to happen.

"I'll get certified to teach high school history in about two years, after I get my B.A. and I'm done with student teaching. I got a chance to work as an assistant coach at my high school this past summer. I loved working with the kids on fundamentals: fielding, bunting, and running the bases. They were eager to learn; it was a real high being their instructor. The coach wants me back after I get certified. I'm really excited.

"There's not much for me to worry about right now. For the first time I don't have to worry about bills or anything. I just have to worry about what I want to do and concentrate on my goals."

⇛ Fight for your vision. ⇚

"I've always been a kind of stubborn person, the kind of person who keeps going," Daniel said. "Things would happen, and I would just say, 'I have to do this.' The only other alternative is giving up, and that was never an option for me. That was the way I saw things. I always believed that I would eventually be able to get what I wanted. I still feel that if you want something and work hard enough, you should be able to do it. And when you do, the harder you've worked, the more rewarding it is.

"Life can get pretty difficult, but you've got to fight through the bad times. You need to have a plan for your life, a dream to hold on to. Otherwise, you'll just float around and get yourself lost. And you need to be willing to work hard. There's always a possibility for success if you're willing to fight for it."

Sculpt Your Personal Masterpiece

Creating a masterpiece is replete with problems. Anything that you can possibly imagine going wrong has, at some point, gotten in the way of someone's masterpiece. And those that today hang in the museum, proud and inspiring, were only realized because those artists fought for their vision.

Those who succeed never run from a challenge. They fight against the odds, just as Michelangelo fought for completing his vision of the Sistine Chapel ceiling despite the pope's wishes.

The fact is, only one person is ever responsible for the success or failure of your vision—you. Realize your personal responsibility and accept the battles that may lie ahead, and you'll be another step closer to bringing your masterpiece to life.

To fight for your vision successfully, you must not only commit to the struggle, but you must also anticipate it. Just as Michelangelo studied his enemies in developing the fortress to protect Florence, you must study your potential barriers to change and develop an innovative strategy to deal with them. Ask yourself these questions as you carry out your plan:

+ What could go wrong in this situation?

+ What are the signs that could point to a potential problem?

+ What in my experience has prepared me to overcome this obstacle?

+ What other resources might I need to overcome this obstacle?

+ What contingency plans can I create to overcome potential obstacles?

Be aware as you fight for your vision that certain obstacles might actually be opportunities in the long term. So be careful before changing course. Unless there is a compelling reason to alter your plan, maintain its integrity and continue the fight for your vision.

Discovery Exercises

1. On a sheet of paper, list the five most important requirements (for example, education, experience, money, skills, family support) for the life change that you're considering.

2. Examine your list. How difficult will each of these requirements be for you to achieve? Assign each a rating from 1 to 10 (with 10 being the most difficult) based on the effort, cost, and time required as well as foreseeable obstacles.

3. Now add up the difficulty ratings for all the tasks (50 points is the highest possible total). The higher the total score, the more difficult it will be to achieve your vision. Any score greater than 25 indicates that you have a hard fight ahead.

4. Next, for each requirement that you gave a rating of 5 or higher, consider the key internal (within you) and external (defined by the situation) obstacles that will make success difficult. If a primary requirement is family support, your key internal obstacle might be your difficulty in standing up for yourself, and your key external obstacle might be prejudice by a family member regarding your chosen career. Or if a primary requirement is analytic skills, your key internal obstacle might be a lifelong fear of mathematics, and your key external obstacle might be a two-

hour commute to attend an appropriate training program. Write down these key internal and external obstacles, and keep them handy as reminders of your impending challenges.

Now prepare! No matter how difficult the road ahead, success is possible, if you're willing to first prepare and then fight.

St. Peter's Basilica
The dome, or cupola, designed by Michelangelo is nearly
four hundred feet tall and served as a model for domes built
centuries later, including the U.S. Capitol in Washington,
D.C.

8

Use Your Unique Experience Creatively

When Michelangelo needed a scaffold built to enable him to paint the ceiling of the Sistine Chapel, Pope Julius called upon Bramante, the leading architect of that period. But Bramante couldn't figure out how to build the scaffold without drilling holes that would damage the fresco. A uniquely innovative solution was required. The matter was brought to the pope for resolution whereupon the pope turned to Michelangelo and said, "Since this won't do, go and build it yourself." Michelangelo dismantled the scaffold, and he recovered so many ropes from it that, when he gave them to a poor assistant of his, the proceeds enabled the man to marry off two of his daughters. Michelangelo built his scaffold without ropes in such a way and so well fitted and joined that the greater the weight upon it, the more secure it became.

—The Life of Michelangelo,
Ascanio Condivi, 1553

The Roman skyline is home to some of architecture's masterpieces: the Colosseum, the Pantheon, the Arch of Constantine. Among these Roman treasures is the magnificent dome of St. Peter's Basilica. Looking now on this iconic structure—upon which the design for the U.S. Capitol was based—it's hard to believe it was almost never completed.

The design for St. Peter's Basilica was begun in 1506 by one of the greatest architects of the Italian Renaissance, Donato Bramante. Unfortunately, Bramante died in 1514, before moving the massive project even close to completion. And what Bramante left in his wake were a beautiful idea and a series of intractable architectural problems, chief among them the construction of the great dome.

In Bramante's plan for the basilica, the dome was to be the building's crowning achievement. Rising high into the heavens, from it one could survey all the Roman landscape from its perfect vantage point. Over the course of the next forty years, pope after pope commissioned architect after architect to finish the basilica that Bramante had set out on paper. One after another, architects attempted to find elegant solutions to the plan's many structural questions. And one after another, architects failed.

And then there were those who didn't try to complete Bramante's design. Thinking they could improve upon the elements and finally get the basilica completed, these architects set out to create their own version of it, but to no avail. They, too, failed and were replaced.

It seemed no architect was up to the task of delivering a design that was both structurally sound and divinely beautiful—that is, until the reign of Pope Paul III.

Pope Paul III understood the type of man needed to complete the difficult job. What he needed was a true creative genius, someone who would take an innovative approach to the structure's vexing problems. What the pope needed was Michelangelo.

Over the years, Michelangelo had often criticized the various designs for the basilica and championed the original design Bramante had laid out.

But one cannot be an armchair architect. To be successful as an architect, one must have an enormous amount of knowledge. Theories of spatial design, functional analysis, project management—the syllabus of the great architect is pages and pages long. Michelangelo had never read a single word of it.

At the time of his appointment, Michelangelo was not even considered to be an architect. There is no record of his formal training in the field. And the limited work he had done, while showing great imagination, usually paired him with a trained architect. Plus, by the time Pope Paul III commissioned the great artist to be the chief architect of St. Peter's, Michelangelo was in his seventies.

Of course, this didn't stop Michelangelo.

We all know what happens next. The pope chooses Michelangelo to complete the work on the basilica. Michelangelo envisions another masterpiece. It all falls into place, as the theme music swells.

But the question remains, how did he do it? How did he master a field despite having no formal training and only limited experience? How did Michelangelo design and build one of the greatest structures in all of Rome?

Michelangelo took what he knew and looked deeper.

Without the ability to connect different experiences, creating a masterpiece is nigh impossible—even if you know what you're doing. Whether it's finding a new solution to a common problem, melding disparate media, creating new forms, or simply viewing a weighty obstacle from another angle, finding the connections in your unique experiences yields the innovations that become masterpieces.

Sounds simple, right? Sorry. Innovating is not a simple task. It requires replacing your old eyes with a new pair, turning your mind upside down, and twisting all you know inside out. And that's never been easy.

To be an innovator, you have to think in ways you've never thought before—or, better, in ways no one's ever thought before. You need to take a close look at all you know, and then somehow look even deeper into that knowledge to find the threads that hold it all together.

> ⇒ *Finding the connections in your unique experiences yields the innovations that become masterpieces.* ⇐

Michelangelo was truly a master at looking deeper, and his passion for in-depth understanding was nowhere in greater evidence than in his studies of the human form, which he viewed as essential to his art.

During his apprenticeship with the master artist Ghirlandaio, Michelangelo was noted for his ability to render the line that brought a human form to life on the page. His early drawings show this ability: the flow of garments, the bulge of muscular flesh, the supple gesture of a woman's hand.

Michelangelo's sculpture shows a similar understanding of line. In his great masterworks, his ability to translate a draft's genitive line into three dimensions is readily apparent. The foreshortening of the bodies in the *Pietà*, the golden proportions of his *David*—all these incredible marble surfaces conceived through the work of the master's chisel.

But Michelangelo was not satisfied with rendering surfaces. He knew there was something deeper, something profound beneath those surfaces that would make his work even more radiant. Beneath the drape of that garment, beneath the veneer of that flesh was God's machine, the engine of life. If Michelangelo was to truly render a human body, he needed to understand the system of form, function, and structure.

Unfortunately, for Michelangelo the only way to see this system was by potentially committing a mortal sin. In Michelangelo's day, human dissection was not generally allowed by the Roman Catholic Church. Michelangelo, intuitively aware of the importance of this knowledge, would not be deterred. He lobbied the church for the privilege of viewing the very workings of life. Through intense efforts, he was granted a special dispensation to dissect bodies that awaited burial in a nearby hospital.

In working with the cadavers, Michelangelo's instincts were proved correct. The understanding of anatomy that he gained through dissection improved his already prodigious drawing skills and ultimately informed his rendering of human form in his great masterpieces.

But would you believe this understanding of anatomy just might have been one of the keys to the problems of St. Peter's Basilica?

Never formally trained, Michelangelo took a sculptural approach to architecture. To do so, he looked deep into his unique body of knowledge and synthesized innovative connections.

As a sculptor Michelangelo understood the physics of stone. From creating the frescoes of the Sistine Chapel, Michelangelo understood how to compose large-scale projects. In building Florence's fortifications, Michelangelo had learned the principles of construction. And of course, his training as an artist had taught him how the interplay of shadow, light, and form created the beautiful.

But the key to conceiving a design for the difficult dome was Michelangelo's understanding of structure. His innovation was to see architectural structure as analogous to the structural elegance of the human system. He looked deeper at his understanding of anatomy and saw its connections to all structural anatomies—including those of a building. The result of his innovative thinking was a structural design so brilliant that it was carried out even years after his death—a fitting legacy for one of history's greatest geniuses.

Ben

It was the last few seconds of the girls' championship soccer game, the big rematch of the previous year's game: West Millburn versus Crestwood. And the game was tied.

Up in the stands, Ben tried to enjoy himself. This was exactly why he had made the transition into his new career: to spend time with his family, to be here watching his daughter, Tessa, the star defender for the Crestwood team, playing against her archrivals.

But while on most days nothing would bring him more joy then seeing Tessa's team win, today Ben had a lot on his mind.

Ben had moved from social work to government, then to investment banking, and now to the creation of low-income housing. He and his partners had launched their new business by reaching out to their families and friends for investments. While this plan had worked out quite well, it also created tremendous pressure for the business to succeed.

As with any investment, particularly a new business, there is a high degree of risk. Add family and friends to the equation, and that risk increases dramatically. For when you take the money of people who are close to you, not only do you risk their hard-earned funds, but you're also risking your most important and profound relationships.

Today, sitting here watching his daughter drive the ball up the field toward the opposing team's goal, he wondered how he could make this new business work.

Ben and his partners had decided to focus on in-town, low-income senior housing. To succeed, they needed projects. And finding projects was extremely difficult, as virtually all the potentially suitable sites had been gobbled up by builders for expensive single-family homes and condos. There appeared to be no land available, even for a modest-sized senior citizen development.

It had been a full quarter since Ben's company had raised its financing, and still they had no prospects. It was no wonder Ben had a lot on his mind.

While Ben was stuck in worry, back on the soccer field, a frustrated shout rang out as Crestwood lost possession of the ball.

Ben snapped to attention and rose from his chair. Seemingly from out of nowhere, a blond lightning bolt of a girl, sporting the unlucky number of thirteen, dribbled down the field, blowing past Tessa and two other Crestwood defenders and breaking toward the goal. When her foot fired, the goalie nearly fell over at the shock of the blow. West Millburn had scored the winning goal.

A roar went up from the West Millburn stands. West Millburn parents joyously rushed onto the field. Ben ran onto the field to comfort Tessa, who was in tears.

On the ride home, Ben didn't mind that the dirt on Tessa's cleats stained the rug of his car. He understood that losing was hard.

At the first red light, he tried to lighten the mood. "You did great, kid. We'll get them next year." Silence. Tessa just stared out the window.

Ben tried a different tack. "Hey, what you looking at, kiddo?"
"Garbage."

"Well, that's nice." Ben looked over his daughter's shoulder and out the window. His eyes nearly popped out of his head.

There, in the middle of the town, was a large expanse of undeveloped land, a "For Sale" sign stuck right in the middle of it. It was a perfect site for senior citizens' housing, and somehow it was right here in the center of West Millburn! The traffic light switched to green as Ben excitedly reached into his glove compartment for a pen.

"Dad! The light's green."

Ben fumbled and finally pulled the pen out and, with car horns blaring behind him, copied the sign's phone number onto the palm of his hand. "What are you doing, Dad?"

"Honey, I know your team lost the game, and, as you might say, it sucks to lose. But trust me, in every cloud there's a silver lining. And I just found it."

>>> *Accept the challenge, even when many others have failed before you.* <<<

That week Jeff, Ben, and Frank began to look into the status of West Millburn. Jeff discovered that West Millburn was not, in fact, meeting its state-mandated requirements for low-income housing, and so he began drafting a complaint, the first step in bringing a lawsuit. And Frank determined that the site was suitable for seniors' housing from a planning perspective.

Ben discovered that the ten acres of land was owned by various members of the Spencer family, who had inherited it twenty years earlier. The broker for the site was unusually honest. He told Ben that the reason the property was still on the market was because the Spencers were a particularly dysfunctional family group. There were twelve of them, none of the members got along, and many of them wouldn't even speak to one another. To sell the property they all had to agree.

"I'm almost ready to give up on this listing," the broker lamented. "No joke. I've had this on the market for three years, and there's been a lot of interest. But it's impossible to get these Spencers to close on a deal when they'd rather torture each other by not signing the contracts."

Ben used his local contacts to find out more about the Spencers. There were loads of stories, and with each new story Ben's heart sank further. He knew this deal was the deal he needed to cut right now. It was the perfect plot of land. It was a community that needed better housing for low-income seniors. It was just the deal his business needed. And it just might be impossible to pull off.

> ⋙ *Look deep into seemingly unrelated past experiences for clues to resolve current dilemmas.* ⋘

I soon found Ben's voice on my phone. He sounded discouraged. "To put together this deal, I'm going to have to somehow get these people who won't even sit in the same room with each other to talk, for hours at a time, no less," Ben told me over the phone. "Nothing in my history of making deals has prepared me for this."

"Well, what about other things in your history? What about your experience outside the world of deal making?"

"Sure. In doing social work, we often had to deal with some difficult people. But I don't think that applies here."

"Are you sure you're looking deep enough at that experience? I mean, you're not just an M.B.A. You have clinical experience in psychological counseling, right?"

"I guess I could sign them up for family counseling, but I am long out of practice. Plus, with this group, a therapeutic breakthrough could take years."

"True. But you didn't get your degree in social work to be a counselor, did you?"

"No, I didn't."

The fact was Ben had done an internship as a mental health counselor but had never practiced professionally. Ben got his M.S.W. in administration for another reason; he realized that the structures that underlay all group relations were psychological in nature. If he could understand these structures and learn better what made people tick, as the executive director of a Lower East Side family program, he could apply this knowledge toward getting his staff to work as a team and strengthening clients' family systems.

"Ben, getting your M.S.W. back then was really innovative. You took a body of knowledge, you looked deeper at it, and you saw a connection to another body of knowledge, business management. It's innovations like these that create masterpieces. What you need right now to solve this problem is another innovative solution. We both know you're capable of that. You just have to look deeper at what you know. Find the connections. For instance, are there lessons in your team-building work that can help you bring the Spencers together to work toward this deal?"

Ben hardly took a beat to think. Score one for our team. "Yes, yes. One of the Spencers was recently divorced, and I know she'll want to sell quickly because she needs money. And she is the only one who has a decent relationship with the elder brother, who has undermined every deal. Maybe if I start with these two, I can generate some momentum for a deal. The trick will be the eldest sister, whose home is on the corner of the property, but maybe I could guarantee her . . ."

Ben stopped, realizing he was giving me more than I would ever need to know about the Spencer family. "Right. Yes. There are lessons there. I think I have a few phone calls to make."

Over the course of the next few months, Ben used his knowledge of psychology, team building, and business to help bring the Spencers toward a contract. Together, we did some role-playing to help him prepare for the calls, focusing on showing real value to each member of the family who was involved in the deal. When they finally appeared in his office to sign the contracts, they may have still been a dysfunctional family, but they all did sign.

For Ben, Jeff, and Frank, it was the first step in a tremendously successful project that enabled them to provide their investors with a sizable profit and leave money over for additional developments. Even more important, Ben had learned to use his unique and varied background to move beyond the surfaces and to synthesize his previous experiences to create innovative solutions.

Drawing once again on both his social work and business backgrounds, Ben helped to create an unusual and exciting low-income senior housing project. The development included a very well-equipped senior center with exercise facilities, arts and crafts rooms, a garden, game rooms, and a variety of other modern features. Moreover, Ben obtained funding for two social workers who were assigned to connect the seniors to each other and to the rest of the community. This resulted in an innovative "grandparenting" program, which got the seniors involved with the children of single-parent families in the neighborhood. And to make the project even more acceptable to the neighbors, Ben and his partners lined up an award-winning architect and landscape designer to ensure that the center wouldn't just be functional—it would be beautiful as well.

Sculpt Your Personal Masterpiece

How did Michelangelo master a field like architecture, a field in which he had no formal training, and somehow, at the age of seventy-one, create the magnificent and lasting design for the dome of St. Peter's Basilica? He looked at all of his knowledge and then looked deeper to find innovative connections in his unique body of experience.

Mastery, after all, isn't just about being competent in your field. It's also about being creative. Mastery is an art! To become a true master, you cannot just amass all the possible knowledge in a chosen field. You also need to create new bodies of knowledge. To do so, you must find the connections between seemingly unrelated matters, like sculpting marble and erecting a dome.

You can call on the knowledge you've gained from everything you've done, from parenting to sales. And the more broadly educated and experienced you are, the more innovating becomes possible.

How? You can jump-start your brain by learning a new skill or honing an old one. If you have hobbies or outside interests, add to your knowledge or skill in that endeavor. Learn to play a musical instrument. Try drawing or photography. Study Portuguese. Or economics. Or neurobiology. Allow yourself extraordinary experiences. Go trekking in China. Attend an opera if you've never been to one. Train for a marathon. Try ethnic foods you've never eaten before. Break your usual patterns and habits.

And all along, as you expand your platform for innovation, look deeper at all you know and have experienced. In looking for opportunities or solving problems in your chosen field, ask yourself these questions:

+ How can I think about this from another perspective?

+ What have I learned from a different experience that might apply here?

+ What is the likely impact of current trends?

+ How did past and contemporary masters in my area of focus innovate and achieve success?

Discovery Exercises

1. Across the top of a blank sheet of paper, list five activities that you spend a substantial amount of time at (for example, parenting, participating in a sport you love, playing a musical instrument, pursuing a favorite hobby, traveling). Under each of these five activities, list as many skills and insights you have gained that you can think of.

2. How might each of these skills and insights add to your ability to find innovative approaches in achieving mastery in your career or another area of your life? Think hard. Be creative. Write your responses using a new sheet of paper for each response. Add to these responses over time as you gain new insights and have additional ideas.

3. Create a plan to involve yourself in new activities, which will enable you to learn new skills and insights. Choose new activities that will wake you up, lead your mind in new directions, and provide you with a larger platform for connecting with people. And the new skills and insights you gain will provide fresh perspectives and added strengths for you to innovate in creating an extraordinary career and life.

You have now taken the first step in achieving mastery in your area of focus as mastery requires not only understanding the current body of knowledge and experience but expanding that body in new and innovative ways.

David (in the plaza)

This statue is a replica of the original *David* in its original location outside the Palazzo Vecchio. The original was moved indoors to the Academia in Florence in 1873.

Photograph by Ken Schuman

9

Push Your Limits

This block of marble was eighteen feet high, and from it, unluckily, one Maestro Simone da Fiesole had begun a giant, and he had managed to work so ill, that he had hacked a hole between the legs, and it was all misshapen and reduced to ruin. Michelangelo resolved to ask for it from Soderini and the Wardens, by whom it was granted to him as a thing of no value. Whereupon Michelangelo made a model of wax, fashioning in it, as a device for the Palace, a young David with a sling in his hand, to the end that, even as he had defended his people and governed them with justice, so those governing that city might defend her valiantly and govern her justly.

—Life of Michelangelo,
Giorgio Vasari, 1568

Michelangelo's *David*—can you picture it standing in the middle of your town?

You're walking down the street. The sun is shining. My, it's a nice day. Maybe you'll get the newspaper and read it in the park. You round a corner and there, in the middle of the town, is the *David*. He looms over you, fourteen feet into the air—the size of a small oak. His eyes cast out over the horizon. He's waiting for something—for the giant, Goliath. And he is ready to do battle.

If you were to come across the *David* just like that, you might begin to understand the power Michelangelo's masterpiece held for the people of Florence.

But let's take a step back for a second. Let's imagine what it was like to be Michelangelo as he sculpted the *David*. The year was 1501, a time of turbulence for the Republic of Florence. The republic, which had been established seven years earlier, was under constant threat of attack and in need of a symbol to serve as a rallying cry for its people. Michelangelo, at the age of twenty-six, was already a widely celebrated sculptor, having completed the *Pietà* a year before. He could have played it safe, working on conventional themes using only marble that he had personally selected with care from the Carrara quarries. But Michelangelo chose to push his limits to test the full power of his art and to assert his patriotic convictions.

So here he now stood. Before him, as he himself described it, his own Goliath—an eighteen-foot block of ruined marble that he would have to conquer.

And when Michelangelo looked inside that damaged stone before him, he had a vision. Inside the misshapen stone, he saw a lightly armed David ready to slay the giant Goliath, his head turned in utmost concentration, his eyes watchful and resolute, his body taut, anticipating combat. The giant was coming, and this David was prepared. This David was a Florence that could overcome all opposition.

At the same time that Michelangelo's *David* was a symbol of Florence, one might also say it stood as a symbol of people's struggles to push beyond their capabilities, to face their own Goliath and, with slingshot in hand and one well-aimed stone, to bring down the unbeatable opponent.

You might say that the story of David and Goliath—and of Michelangelo's creation of the *David*—is the story of anyone who pursues his or her personal masterpiece. For what is creating a masterpiece but taking on the biggest challenges—with the biggest risks and fears—and conquering them one by one?

Jack

After Jack helped win the fight to save Silver Forest, he knew this wasn't the last battle. Preservation in his town was an ongoing struggle.

From his current work at the land trust, Jack learned a great deal about the trends affecting his county. New train lines throughout the state were shortening commutes. As the train lines became available, commuters in more densely populated suburban areas moved farther north, into Jack's county. In the communities surrounding Jack's town, acres of fir trees were soon replaced with McMansions and strip malls. And Jack's town was next.

While Jack and his group had stopped Silver Forest, they knew they couldn't stop every large-scale development under the current zoning laws. Because of the way these laws were written in Jack's community, it was quite easy for developers to take over plots of untouched land. It seemed the only way to hold off the encroachment of rapid development in this rural environment was to be in a position to change the laws.

The way to win that fight was clear. Someone with a preservation mind-set had to be elected to public office. What Jack's town needed was an environmentalist mayor.

The town's charter permitted the mayor to serve only a single six-year term. And it just so happened that the sixth year of the current mayor's term had just begun.

Jack saw an opportunity. After having successfully fought for preserving Silver Forest, he had a unique platform in his community. Everyone in the town knew Jack. Almost everyone in the town liked Jack, even if they didn't always agree with what he believed. On top of this, everyone knew that Jack produced results.

⇶ *Feeling that you are making a difference helps you push your boundaries.* ⇷

Jack's campaign for mayor was well organized and well funded. Donations came in from the chapter of his environmental group and the many people in town whom Jack inspired by standing up against the town council.

Drawing on his strengths in marketing and communications, Jack was able to deliver a focused and clear message to the community. And his promotional materials, while inexpensive, were extremely professional.

But it wasn't all just gloss. Jack campaigned aggressively. Jack's friends in the environmental group took to the streets and proselytized. Jack went on his own baby-kissing and hand-shaking tour, personally knocking on the door of every house in the town.

As the leaves turned orange and brown on the trees, Jack's son and his young friends rode their mountain bikes through the town with "Jack for Mayor" banners flying from their handlebars. Jack watched as they rode down the sun-dappled main street. "This is going to be easy," he thought to himself.

On the night of the election, Jack and his wife went to cast their ballots at the local elementary school. Jack brought his son into the ballot booth with him and showed him how the machine worked. Jack lifted his son up and allowed him to select his choice for mayor.

That night Jack and his wife sat on their couch watching the national election results on the television. As the candidate they favored for governor lost the election, Jack cursed to himself. His wife turned to him. "What happens if you lose, Jack?"

"We're not going to lose."

"What if you do? You should know that you ran a good campaign. You've raised people's consciousness of the issues. People really believe in you."

"We're not going to lose."

At 6 A.M. Jack awoke from his position on the couch. There was a kink in his neck. His foot was asleep. "Got to get to work," he thought.

And then the phone rang. Jack hobbled to the phone. It was his campaign manager—and the news wasn't good. Jack had lost the election.

Jack found some solace in the fact that by working for the land trust, which bought untouched wilderness in order to preserve it from development, he was doing his part to save the environment. Jack loved his work. He loved feeling a part of a movement. He loved feeling that his work was making a difference in this world. But it wasn't all clear sailing.

⟫⟫ *Pushing your limits involves sacrifice.* ⟪⟪

Jack had to sacrifice many things to work in this field. He sacrificed his title and nearly $80,000 a year in salary. He sacrificed vacations and new clothes. In a lot of ways, he had sacrificed the entirety of his previous career track. He was, in effect, starting again at the bottom of the ladder. This was not where Jack wanted to be.

Anyone who rallies a community against powerful government forces has ambitions. Even in his other career as a marketing and communications specialist, Jack showed ambition. He worked his way up the ladder from being an English lit graduate to a marketing director.

But Jack wasn't just ambitious, he performed. He was capable, driven, and persistent; he had what it takes to realize his ambitions—even when they were not exactly aligned with his values.

Now Jack's ambitions niggled at his brain. Looking up from the bottom of the land trust ladder, Jack saw the possibility of being at the top. He was certainly capable of being there one day. He learned his job quickly and developed strong skills from working closely with the executive director.

On top of this, Jack began to understand the workings of the land trust and the larger not-for-profit world. Unfortunately, Jack began to understand that in small not-for-profit organizations like the land trust, there was little room for growth.

The director of his organization was also its founder. Beyond her leadership there was no real hierarchical structure. And while the challenges of the land trust position allowed him to be stimulated by his job and to take plenty of responsibility, it would never allow him to realize his ambitions and his family's financial security, including looming college costs for his two children.

So while Jack knew he wanted to be a mover and a shaker in the environmental preservation world, he had no idea how he was going to get there. And he also didn't have time. He was not a young man, after all, and he didn't want to wait for ten years to attain the position he truly desired. There was no guarantee that he would achieve his dream even if he put in the time.

The not-for-profit world was a world of influence and connections, not just within one's particular enterprise but in the outside world as well—in town councils, state and federal government, philanthropy, corporations, and developers. Jack got the picture. If he was going to become the executive director of an environmental organization, he would need to lay some groundwork.

>>> *To combat your deepest fear,*
you need to confront your Goliath. <<<

When Jack and I discussed his situation, it became clear there was one sure way to gain influence and prominence: run for public office again in his community, but this time, win. When we came to this realization, Jack started to fidget in his seat.

"Something about this thought is making you uncomfortable," I remarked.

"You remember how I told you about running for mayor after Silver Forest. You remember I lost?"

"So? That was a few years back. And you don't have to run for mayor."

"I know. But I don't know how comfortable I am with putting myself out there again. It's not easy. It takes a lot of energy."

"Of course."

"And it's not really my sweet spot. I mean, I'm no politician."

Jack was certainly giving me a lot of reasons why he couldn't do it, but I wasn't convinced. In my mind, he hadn't really given me the real reason why he wasn't going to run. I would have to give it to him myself. "This is your Goliath, isn't it?"

"Huh?"

"It's your Goliath: the challenge that scares you, the battle you don't think you can win."

"It's true. I'm scared of putting all that effort in and losing again."

"Then that's exactly what you need to do. The moment you feel uncomfortable is the moment before you make a breakthrough. If you want to create your masterpiece, you need to take on Goliath. If you don't, you'll fail without even trying. If you do, you just might realize that Goliath isn't so big."

Jack resolved that day to give it a shot. It was nearly spring. There were eight months until November and the elections that would determine two open town council seats. Jack would have to move quickly if his name was going to be on the ballot.

Things progressed smoothly with his campaign. Jack rather quickly amassed the signatures he needed to get on the ballot. He was again able to rally support from the environmental groups he worked with in the area, as well as from his close friends. And again, his strength in marketing and communications served him well, as he was able to convey a strong, consistent message to the community.

But what he found most uncomfortable was knocking on the doors.

Of course, Jack realized the importance of getting his face in front of everyone in the town. It was a public relations must in a town of a few thousand people, where it was actually possible to shake the hand of every voter. It simply required going door-to-door.

What made this most uncomfortable for Jack was the fact that he had knocked on many of these doors just a few years before. Now many of those in his community opened their doors and saw a loser.

"Running for office again, Jack?" they'd say. "Wasn't once enough?" The comments cut Jack to the core, and often he found his heart racing before his hand reached for the doorbell.

But Jack knew that he had to take this step in order to defeat his Goliath and ultimately achieve his goal. So to combat his fear, each time he got to a particularly difficult door and his heart began to race, he took a deep breath and reminded himself why he was knocking—to preserve his town's natural beauty.

When November rolled around, the leaves fell from the trees in Jack's backyard and spread across the lawn. Jack hurriedly raked them into piles amidst juggling work and the campaign. The vote was coming.

He telephoned supporters and drove people to the polls. He was determined that, having come this far, he would win.

That night, exhausted, Jack sat next to his wife and watched the election results. As he dozed on the couch, his wife elbowed him when a congresswoman they were supporting was reelected. "Harbinger of things to come?" she asked.

"I don't want to hold my breath."

The phone rang at 6 A.M. Usually when the phone rings at that hour, something terrible has happened. Or something great. Jack jumped up from bed at the sound of the ring and reached for the phone. The voice on the other end had only questions.

"Jack?"

"Yes."

"Hal Jefferson from the *Silver County News*. What's your statement upon winning the town council election?"

Jack stuttered, "I'm sorry, but did you just say, winning?"

"Yes. What is your statement?"

"One moment." Jack couldn't contain his excitement. He put down the phone and shook his wife. "We won!" Jack's wife threw her arms around her husband.

Jack turned back to the reporter on the phone. "My statement? I thank the voters of Silver County for their trust in me. And I'm going to take on anyone who wants to replace the beauty of our town with a strip mall."

⋙ *Success breeds success.* ⋘

During his term on the town council, Jack learned how to work with developers to find alternate sites with less negative environmental impact. And he ended up meeting and building relationships with government officials in other towns and on a state level. He even had dinner with the governor, when he was named by a newspaper as one of the state's most important environmental activists.

All this attention got Jack noticed, not just by the people of his town but by those in the field of environmental preservation. At the end of his council term, Jack began to again float his résumé. He was surprised when he applied for a midlevel position at a particular preservation organization and got a call asking him to interview for another position, executive director.

Today Jack directs an organization that is devoted to maintaining wetlands and coastal areas in his state. He nearly doubled his salary, and while it's still less than he made with the accounting firm, he lives quite comfortably and happily. Each new day gives him the opportunity to do what he loves—contributing to preserving the environment and making a difference in the quality of life for the residents of his state, for his children, and for his future grandchildren.

No, his work isn't easy. It's a constant battle. And sometimes when dealing with the factions that oppose him, Jack feels scared. Sometimes the battle seems unwinnable; sometimes his opponents seem too big and powerful; sometimes history seems against him; sometimes there seems to be no real hope. But each time Jack gets these feelings in his gut, he remembers one thing: Goliath isn't so big.

The Truth About the Sistine Chapel

When you look at the sheer scale of the frescoes on the Sistine Chapel ceiling, with its elaborately detailed iconography and vibrant colors, energy seemingly emanating from each brushstroke, you have to imagine Michelangelo created this masterpiece in a state of bliss. You have to imagine that the work flowed like magic from Michelangelo's brush. You have to imagine that the creation of those frescoes was an act of divine grace and a glorious, peak experience for the artist.

And you'd be absolutely wrong.

The truth is that Michelangelo didn't want to paint the Sistine Chapel ceiling and, in fact, painted it in extreme physical distress.

According to his contemporary biographer, Giorgio Vasari, Michelangelo was coerced into working on the Sistine Chapel through the insidious efforts of enemies seeking to undermine his reputation. In other words, one of the greatest masterpieces ever created began as a setup.

Some of the most important artists in Rome were jealous of Michelangelo's ability to create masterpieces in sculpture "at which they saw him to be perfect," according to Vasari, and of the high regard in which he was held by Pope Julius II. They convinced the pope to assign to Michelangelo the task of painting the vast Sistine Chapel ceiling with the expectation that he would fail, which would "plunge him into despair." Vasari writes, "They thought that if they compelled him to paint, he would do work less worthy of praise, since he had no experience of colors in fresco, and that he would prove inferior to Raphael."

For his part, Michelangelo begged the pope to allow him to continue working on the pope's colossal tomb, for which Michelangelo was supposed to create more than forty statues. Vasari continues,

"Michelangelo, who desired to finish the tomb, believing the vaulting of that chapel to be a great and difficult labor, and considering his own want of practice in colors, sought by any means to shake such a burden from his shoulders, and proposed Raphael for the work. But the more he refused, the greater grew the desire of the Pope, who was headstrong in his undertakings."

>>> *When faced with an unpleasant task,*
don't just go through the motions. <<<

Michelangelo foresaw the ordeal that was coming his way with the Sistine Chapel. If anything, though, the actual experience was even worse than the nightmare he had expected. He described what it was like in a satirical sonnet that he wrote to his friend Giovanni d'Pistoia.

> This comes of dangling from the ceiling—
> I'm goitered like a Lombard cat
> (or wherever else their throats grow fat)—
> it's my belly that's beyond concealing,
> it hangs beneath my chin like peeling.
> My beard points skyward, I seem a bat
> upon its back, I've breasts and splat!
> On my face the paint's congealing.
>
> Loins concertina'd in my gut,
> I drop an arse as counterweight
> and move without the help of eyes.
> Like a skinned martyr I abut
> On air, and, wrinkled, show my fate.
> Bow-like, I strain towards the skies.

No wonder then I size
things crookedly; I'm on all fours.
Bent blowpipes send their darts off-course.
Defend my labour's cause,
good Giovanni, from all strictures:
I live in hell and paint its pictures.

For four years, Michelangelo worked cramped upon the elaborate scaffolding he had erected to enable him access to the soaring ceiling. Most of the time, Michelangelo stood high above the ground, his back arched in a painful curve, his vision strained, toxic paint dripping in his eyes. For Michelangelo, the joy of painting gave way to back spasms.

Michelangelo was no glutton for punishment. He preferred the controlled working environment of his beloved sculpture studio. But he understood responsibility. He understood that when there is something you ought to do, you should throw yourself into it and do it right. So when required by the pope, God's representative on Earth, to take on the responsibility of painting the ceiling of the Sistine Chapel for the greater glorification of God, Michelangelo determined not just to go through the motions but to create a masterpiece.

The Truth About Your Masterpiece

Some call it flow. Some call it being in the zone. Others don't have a name for it, but they know it when they feel it. Whatever you call it, it's that feeling you get when you're creating something amazing. And doesn't it feel good? And wouldn't it be nice to always feel like that when you're working on your masterpiece?

But sometimes while pursuing your masterpiece, you may feel that nature itself is set against you. No matter how strong your conviction, no matter the depth of your talent, nothing goes your way. In less than six months, your big job becomes a handful of worthless stock options and a small severance check. You're running late for the big meeting, so you take the shortcut but then get lost, arriving even later. You train for months for the Boston Marathon but sprain your ankle at the firing of the starter's gun.

And sometimes life defines your task for you. And like Michelangelo's Sistine Chapel ceiling, your sense of responsibility requires you to channel your efforts in a new direction. You put your career on hold while you raise your children; you volunteer to defend your country; or you invite your aged, ailing parent to finish her years in your home.

Heather

Heather laughed a lot. That was the first thing I noticed about her when I met her in my office two years ago. She had a big, pleasant laugh for things that amused her and a small, nervous laugh often accompanied her more serious observations.

That first meeting called for mostly serious observations as Heather was deciding whether to move her mother, Agnes, into her own home or into a nursing home.

Agnes was ninety-three years old. For the past ten years she had been living in a seniors' apartment that came with lots of support services, organized trips, and built-in companionship. This enabled Agnes to continue living independently although her health had been in gradual but steady decline.

Over the last year she was getting too frail to cook and participate in the planned events. Heart problems, diabetes, and early stages of dementia began to affect her ability to live alone. She'd mostly just eat breakfast but not other meals. Heather would bring over specially cooked food, which she'd later find left uneaten in the refrigerator.

But it wasn't this gradual decline that created the need to consider a nursing home. It was rather a sudden health crisis that no one had expected. While Agnes was reading in her favorite easy chair, she felt a pain in her chest and couldn't breathe. She crawled to a phone while trying to maintain consciousness. Help arrived just in time, and she was rushed to the hospital, where they found she had suffered a minor heart attack.

Agnes was about to transfer to a rehab facility for a two-week stay. But then what? It was clear that her days of living on her own were behind her.

⋙ *Be your best self.* ⋘

No matter what the decision, Heather knew her life was about to change dramatically. She and her mother had been close but relatively independent. Now Heather would have to get much more involved. She felt that she owed it to her mother for the loving care Heather had received as a child.

Agnes was orphaned at the age of twelve. Her own mother had died from complications of appendicitis when Agnes was ten years old, and her father died two years later from cancer. So Agnes went to live with Aunt Mae, who was caring for an ailing older sister. Agnes stayed with her aunt until she married Jim, her high school sweetheart.

Agnes and Jim bought a small house in Maspeth, Queens, and Aunt Mae, who had been like a mother to her, came to live with them. Agnes and Jim started to raise their family. In quick sequence they had two daughters, Heather and Jane, who became the center of Agnes's life. She had lost her own parents early and wanted her children to grow up in a "real family."

Agnes believed in hard work and sacrifice and passed these virtues on to her children. She saw her kids through all the childhood diseases, plus some broken bones, a bout of rubella, and even a polio scare.

"We were the family that everyone brought their stray animals to because they knew we would take them in," Heather told me at one of our meetings. "We would always be available to babysit when someone was going through a hard time. They would just drop their kids off at our house if they needed to. That's kind of what you did. You cared for someone else's kids in hard times and tried to help them through. One of my sister's friends, whose parents were alcoholics, practically lived with us.

"Mom sounds like she was no fun at all. Not true. She made every occasion special for all of us—our birthdays in particular. Mom would serve a great meal and make a big production of bringing out the cake and blowing out the candles. We'd then play charades and other games. Everybody really got into it. Finally, we would do a roast of whoever's birthday it was. And Mom had her turn being roasted just like everyone else." Heather smiled broadly and started to sing, " 'You're a grand old bag, you're a high flying bag.' Mom laughed as hard as anyone else. And any gaffe—like if you fell off a chair—someone would write a song about it. We had lots of fun growing up, and Mom was the center of much of it."

Heather married Bob, whom she met at college while studying psychology. Bob was in the ROTC, and he was sent to Vietnam for the last year of his tour of duty with the Army. On Bob's return, he and Heather moved into the rental apartment in her parents' two-family home.

After Bob got a job working at IBM as a systems analyst, he and Heather could afford to contribute to the rent and save for a home of their own. A year later, they found a small house that they loved, though they weren't sure they could afford it. Heather's parents surprised them with a gift—returning to them all their rental payments.

"We couldn't believe it," Heather related. "They had been putting away all the money we had paid, and they gave it back to us. Sacrifice and family, I got this from the way I was raised."

By then Heather had begun working as a high school guidance counselor. It was a job she committed to with passion. "I wanted to help struggling kids and their parents," she said. "I care a lot about that. And God knows, much of what the students or parents bring up, I've been through myself or with my kids. The hardest part was dealing with the mushrooming caseload as the schools expanded and the number of counselors was cut back. I don't think I could have survived if I weren't pretty well organized. I've even become a lot better at structuring my time. I had to."

Heather and I discussed the options for how and where her mother would live. "How about your sister?" I asked. "Could she help?"

"No, she's on the West Coast, struggling with a big family of her own."

"Anyone else?"

"Not really," she replied. "We are a small family and don't really have much to fall back on."

So our focus was on what Heather could do for her mother and how her decision would relate to her values, passions, and strengths.

After a few meetings, we determined that Heather's primary value was family, her passion was helping people, and her talent was organization. At the nexus of these lay great power and energy. But would these traits be enough for Heather to take on the enormous responsibility of caring for her aged mother while holding a job and dealing with the needs of her marriage and children?

Heather wavered. She had a friend at work who, when faced with this choice, had put her mother in a nursing home. Heather decided to talk to her about that decision. "My friend told me that her mother had suffered miserably in the nursing home—it was a totally demeaning experience. She said that she would regret that decision to her dying day. That inspired me to find the strength to have Mom stay with me."

>>> *Don't underestimate the task ahead.* <<<

I coached Heather once a week for eighteen months, until her mother passed away in Heather's arms at the age of ninety-five. Like Michelangelo and the Sistine Chapel ceiling, the difficulties Heather imagined that she would encounter were dwarfed by the immensity of the actual task. Her experience was so extraordinary that I asked her if I could share it with future clients considering the same decision. Here is how Heather described her experience.

"I worked at the school all day. Bob worked from home as a consultant in information technology. So during the day, Bob was on the front line with Mom. By the time I got home, he had had it and eagerly turned her over to me. After a while, I was exhausted.

"I began to look forward to getting out for short respites. I stopped in the supermarket on my way home. I used to dislike food shopping. But I began to view it as a wonderful thing. I said to myself, 'This is my time for me.' Hard to believe, but shopping for food was my recreation.

"When I got home, I did whatever was needed. Going from one chore to another, to dinner, to cleaning up, to taking Mom to the bathroom, and then going to bed.

"Then Mom fell and broke her shoulder. She was wheelchair bound, which made everything even more difficult. There was very little downtime. The one saving grace was that when I went to bed I was so exhausted I fell right to sleep.

"On the weekends it was worse. Bob often traveled and did presentations. So I had the full responsibility.

"There were endless visits to doctors. I kept a 'Mom book,' in which I recorded her doctor and emergency room visits, her prescriptions, and conversations I had with the doctors. I'm a big believer in writing things down. Often one doctor didn't know what the other had done. And sometimes they disagreed on what to do. So I had to keep abreast of who prescribed what and keep everyone informed.

"We had a whole retinue of people coming in: the home health aides, the nurses, the physical therapist. And it wasn't always the same person, so I had to keep everyone coordinated.

"She took at least eight different pills daily: blood thinner, blood pressure pill, diabetes pill, heart pill, vitamins, and pain pills. Bob and I had to organize and dispense her drugs. Some were twice a day, others three times, and some were every other day. I would call the pharmacy to renew the pills. Bob would supervise the pill taking in the morning, and I would take over when I got home. I made a six-by-eight card with everything written down so I could just hand it to her attendants on hospital visits.

"They would always take her blood pressure when we got to the hospital or the doctor's office. It was always great—120 over 80. One day I asked them to take mine, which had been perfectly normal before I started caring for her. Wouldn't you know—mine had become dangerously high, 160 over 95!"

>>> *Find time to care for your most important needs.* <<<

"I needed to begin caring for myself a bit, so I started on pills myself to keep my blood pressure down. And the doctor cautioned that I needed to find a real break or I would get sick myself and be of no use to anyone. I started singing once a week in my church choir and went to yoga on Monday nights. These were two things that kept me sane. They were two hours each and kind of set the pace for the week. And it was solely for me. I could relax and breathe and maintain my sanity a bit.

"A lot of things went by the wayside. The house, for instance—not that I am a meticulous housekeeper. Anything that was not essential didn't get done. I didn't do much cooking. We often had take-out. I would look for things that she could eat. Soft things, even baby food."

⫸ Brace yourself for the tough parts. ⫷

"It was so hard to watch her deteriorate. I tried to remember the times that she was Mom and all the fun stuff. I asked myself, 'How much longer can I do this?'

"Work was actually a godsend. It helped keep me sane because I couldn't be moping around. It gave me other things to think about. I had to focus on what I had to do that day—if there was a kid who needed me or a parent conference that I needed to go to. My boss and coworkers all knew and were very supportive. If I had to leave early, to take care of a mom emergency, it was never a problem. The parents also understood. Everyone was understanding.

"Toward the end, when she was really uncomfortable, she could be extremely difficult. I put a lot on Bob, who was very helpful. But she was hard on him—demanding and critical—and wouldn't cut him a break. She and Bob would sometimes really go at it.

"And she and I had our share of fights, particularly over her bedtime. This was a real role reversal from when I was a kid. Exhausted, I would try to start readying her for bed at 10 P.M., and she would fight me for an extra half hour.

"She wanted me to sit with her when I had so much else to do. We'd fight over that, too. She would try to get me to watch Lawrence Welk reruns on television with her; it was one of the things she loved from the old days. I generally refused because that was an hour when she was occupied and I could do other things.

"What would really tick me off would be that Mom would get confused and call me by my sister's name or say I was 'the other Heather.' I would respond, 'I know it seems like there are two Heathers because I'm doing so much. But there is only one. There's one Heather who goes to work and one Heather who takes care of you.'

"I look back at it, and I don't know how I did it. The end came pretty quickly. After she fell again on Christmas day, I noticed a steady deterioration. She could hardly feed herself and had difficulty swallowing. Her body was breaking down.

"She said to me, 'I don't want to die, but I don't want to live like this. I'm waiting for God to take me. I don't know why he hasn't.' I could see her pulling away from life in general."

Heather stopped talking at this point. There were tears in her eyes. I clicked off the recorder, and we sat quietly for a while. I asked if there was anything she would have done differently or any advice she would give to others.

"I have regrets," she said thoughtfully. "That I could have been kinder, that I could have sat with her more. That I could have asked her more questions about her life. Because those were the kindnesses that she noticed.

"My experience with my mother reminds me of the story of Jesus in Gethsemane. My mother kept saying, 'Just stay with me.' And that's what Jesus said to the disciples. 'Just stay with me. Can't you keep awake just another hour? I'm going through this agonizing thing. I know I'm going to die, and you can't even keep awake with me.' It's kind of like that. She knows she's going and yet everyone's rushing around. 'What is more important than just sitting with me, holding my hand, and letting me know that you're here with me?'

"That's the only thing I would say to people. Whatever your situation, try to spend time. Show that they mean something to you."

"Do you think that your mother felt cared for?" I asked.

"I think that Mom really did feel loved. That last day when I came in, she gave me this really big smile, and I said 'I love you.' And I kissed her. And she was trying to mouth the words." Tears welled up in Heather's eyes again. "I just wish that I could have been a little more patient," she said softly.

⋙ *It's worth the effort to push your limits.* ⋘

"But you were there when she really needed you," I reminded Heather. "She lived her last years with dignity, surrounded by people she loved. You created that possibility for her. What a precious gift that was."

Heather brightened, reflecting on her accomplishment. "You know, more than seventy people came to Mom's memorial service," she said. "My sister, daughter, and I gave reminiscences. Bob used his skills in digital photography to create a slide show that documented her life, complete with period music. My son sang and played her favorite song on his guitar. After we were done, people—more than a dozen of them—spontaneously got up and told stories about her. Many of the stories were very funny. It was strange to laugh at a memorial service—but wonderful, too. Finally, one of her dear friends who was in her nineties came up and told me, 'When I go, I want to go like this!' In that moment I knew it was worth it. Mom was quite a woman, and she deserved the best I could give," she said thoughtfully.

Sculpt Your Personal Masterpiece

Mastery isn't a state of mind. It's not a buzzword. And it's certainly not an intangible quality that only pertains to a few geniuses who lived in sixteenth-century Italy.

Mastery is an art. It's a way of living that requires creativity, strategy, and faith. It's about pushing your limits. It's the practice of taking on the biggest challenges and risking even bigger failures.

And isn't it time for you to live your life like a master?

No? Perhaps the most likely reason so few answer that question in the affirmative is fear. We're all afraid of failure—the more public that failure, the scarier.

What separates the Michelangelos from journeymen and journeywomen is that willingness to risk failure by pushing their limits. If Michelangelo simply had worked at his most comfortable level, would we have the Sistine Chapel ceiling, the *Pietà*, the *David*, and the dome of St. Peter's Basilica?

To realize any vision, you must at some point take the unworkable slab and pull the *David* from it. You must put yourself on display, get knocked down, and then step up again. You must push yourself. You must take risks.

But risk wisely. There is a big difference between risky and reckless. That difference is in the balance of risk against reward. The riskier the decision—the larger your Goliath—the more careful you should be in considering this balance and the more advance planning you should be doing to mitigate that risk.

Ask yourself these questions:

+ Is this risk real? Or do I just perceive the risk out of fear?

+ Do I need to take this risk to realize my vision?

- What is the worst possible thing that can happen if I take the risk? What is the likelihood of that happening? Could I withstand such an eventuality?

- What is the absolute best thing that could happen?

- And what is the risk if I do nothing?

Discovery Exercises

1. Take a blank sheet of paper, and list the risks required for you to achieve your extraordinary life. For each risk write the answers to the preceding questions.

2. Considering the risk-reward balance, formulate and write down a strategy for dealing with that risk. For example, if the risk is loss of income for an extended period, might there be loans available from banks or family members? Could you cut back your expenses to meet the decline in income? Can you create a reserve now to deal with this possibility?

3. For which of these risks will you need additional support to address (additional financing, special knowledge or skills, additional staff, and so on)? What will be the difficulty in obtaining that support should you require it? How much of that support can you prearrange for should you need it?

By writing down the risks and assessing the impact and potential rewards for each risk, you have gained a better understanding of, and remedies for, the obstacles that might slow your progress. You may still have concerns, but you will have ferreted out unfounded fears that could have derailed you.

Moses

Michelangelo thought that the statue of Moses, the centerpiece for the tomb of his patron, Pope Julius II, was his most lifelike sculpture. Legend has it that Michelangelo was so overwhelmed by the masterpiece he threw his chisel at the statue while imploring "Why don't you talk?" causing a chip in the knee that is visible today.

Photograph by Ron Paxton

10
················
Live with Integrity

Being asked by a friend what he thought of one who had counterfeited in marble some of the most celebrated antique figures and boasted that his imitations had surpassed the antiques by a great measure, Michelangelo replied: "He who goes behind others can never go in front of them, and he who is not able to work well for himself cannot make good use of the works of others."

—Life of Michelangelo,
Giorgio Vasari, 1568

Integrity comes from the root word *integer*, meaning "whole." It involves being integrated whereby all parts are interrelated and unified. Morally, integrity requires adherence to your principles, however uncomfortable that may be.

Michelangelo had integrity. He was committed to following his principles and to making all his life work a unified whole. That does not mean his life was easy or always happy. It means that Michelangelo created a life that fit Michelangelo.

>>> *Having a life of integrity*
requires creating a life that fits you. <<<

For Michelangelo to live a life of integrity, he needed to integrate his passion for art, his religious principles, his patriotism, and his concerns for his family. We've discussed earlier how Michelangelo was able to channel his art, religion, and patriotism through his work. Now let's focus on his family responsibilities.

For many of his contemporaries, Michelangelo was not an easy person to get along with. He had a tendency to be reclusive, mistrustful, and combative. But he was extremely loyal to those who were close to him. Hundreds of letters from Michelangelo to his father, brothers, nephews, and nieces exist, so we have a very good idea of his relationships with them. It is clear from these letters that Michelangelo cared deeply for his family and took his responsibility for their well-being very seriously.

The Buonarroti family had aspirations. Michelangelo's family could trace its ancestors back to the early twelfth century and claimed descent from the counts of Canossa. We saw this family pride in the dissatisfaction of Michelangelo's father when his son chose to be a low-status artist rather than join the wool or silk guilds.

The Buonarroti family had earned its livelihood primarily from the wool trade and money changing but was experiencing hard times as the Renaissance approached. Ludovico, Michelangelo's father, was a podesta, which in modern times would have been a circuit court judge. He traveled to small towns outside of Florence and also collected rents from a few small properties in Florence as well as from a farm in nearby Settignano that he and his older brother had inherited.

Michelangelo was the only one of the Buonarroti children to do well financially. His father and his four brothers were in constant financial difficulty. His nieces lacked dowries, and his nephews required financial support. Michelangelo took responsibility for helping all of them.

But they repeatedly tested his patience (not Michelangelo's strong suit to begin with) and invariably thwarted his hopes for them.

Michelangelo's younger brother, Giovanisimone, was always cooking up grandiose schemes to get rich. Michelangelo had set him up in a wool shop, but Giovanisimone was planning on risking everything on a commercial shipping venture to India. When Michelangelo discovered this, he wrote:

> Giovanisimone: For twelve years now I've been traipsing around Italy, borne all kinds of disgrace, suffered every calamity, lacerated my body with cruel toil, put my own life in danger a thousand times, only to help my family; and now that I've started to raise our house up again a little, just you alone wish to be the one to confound it and ruin in an hour what I've achieved after so many years and through such great toil.

In addition to financial support, Michelangelo tried to provide moral support to his family. While working on the Sistine Chapel ceiling in Rome and awaiting belated payment from the pope, Michelangelo wrote to his father:

> Very dear father: I have given to Giovanni Balducci here 350 broad florins in gold, for him to pay you there. . . . I suffer very much that I cannot help you in any other way. Don't be frightened because of that, and don't give yourself the least distress, because if we lose property, we don't lose life. I shall provide you with more than what you lose, but I must remind you, don't treat it as precious, since it's all an illusion. So do your work, and thank God that since this trouble had to come, it came at a time when you could help yourselves better than you could in the past. Attend to living and let property go sooner than discomforts, for I would rather have you alive and poor, for if you were dead, I wouldn't care for all the gold in the world.

Michelangelo not only took responsibility for his father and brothers but also for his brothers' children. He bought them homes in Florence and farms in Chianti. He provided funds to set them up as shop owners. And he played the role of wise uncle, advising them on everything from investments to marriage.

If Michelangelo had not taken the time to deal with his family's problems, he would still have been a great artist, honoring God with his wondrous masterpieces. But he would not have honored himself. For to live with integrity requires that you integrate all of your most important parts.

⇛ *Don't try to be like Mike.* ⇚

Everybody's different. The life that fit Michelangelo would not likely fit you. Some people need a balance of work and play to achieve a life that fits them. Others need to be helping the poor. Still others need to share the knowledge they have gained by becoming teachers. Use the Michelangelo Method to go as deeply into your true self as you can. Find your values, passions, and strengths there. Create positive goals and commit to pursuing them. Live with integrity.

Susan

I hadn't seen Susan, the legal assistant turned teacher, for three years when she called. She said she needed to see me. I was between client calls and wasn't able to find out more, but we made an appointment for her to come in the following week.

"How's your work going?" I asked after she had settled into a large chair across from mine.

"It's fine. I'm teaching biology at South Side High School. I've gotten really good evaluations. I love the kids, though some of them can be very difficult at times. But I'm honest with them and they like that. And I'm making a difference in their lives by helping them to be more aware and appreciate nature's beauty and to be more respectful of the environment."

"Well, that's great! It seems like you found your proper place. So what brings you here?" I asked.

>> *Understand who you are, but be open to embrace change.* <<

"I'm very happy with my work. Now I'd like to focus on improving my relationships—not just improving, but transforming them. For one thing, I'd like to move ahead with my sisters. Since my father died last year, we've been fighting. I want to become closer with them."

"Were you close with your dad?" I asked.

"We were very close. My mom was institutionalized during my childhood, so my dad raised us. He was always struggling to make ends meet; it was very tough for him. He loved us in his own way, but he felt that being strong meant not expressing your feelings. So we never really were sure where we stood with him. Maybe that's why expressing who I am has become so important to me."

"How old was he when he passed away?" I asked.

"Seventy-four. When he was diagnosed with pancreatic cancer, I was devastated. My sisters were living out of the area. So it fell to me to take care of him—and I wanted to. He was in and out of the hospital all year. In the end, he wanted to die in his own bed, so I took him out of the hospital against his doctor's orders."

"That must have been hard for you," I said.

"Very. In the taxi on the way home dad was so feeble, I thought he would die in my arms. We were both very quiet the whole way, which is unusual for me. But I was so upset I couldn't get any words out. As we were arriving he looked up at me and said, 'Honey, I know that whatever you do, you're going to be a great success.'"

At this point tears welled up in Susan's eyes.

"To finally get that affirmation from him—that he knew I was a capable person and could take care of myself. It was such an inspiring moment for me. I think about it all the time."

She got quiet and said, "He died two days later. And then my sisters started in with me."

"How so?" I asked.

"Well, they resented my dad paying off my credit card debt, which I ran up after I quit my job so that I could care for him. I didn't ask him to, but he insisted. I was really offended by their reaction."

"Have you let them know how you felt about their resentment?"

"No, I haven't yet."

"Why not?"

"I guess I'm afraid of their anger."

"What would be the probable outcome if you never mentioned that to them? Would they resent you more, the same, or less?"

"I imagine that their resentment might actually grow."

"And how would you feel if you never mentioned it to them?"

"Probably worse because I would have to look at myself in the mirror every day and look at an inauthentic person. I definitely have to have that conversation with them," she said firmly. "I'll call them this week."

Be authentic.

Susan and I spent the remainder of our meeting role-playing the conversation she intended to have with her sisters. As we rehearsed, she became more and more comfortable and was looking forward to having an authentic conversation with each of her sisters. In wrapping up the meeting, I acknowledged her commitment to her integrity, her awareness of her behavior and the behavior of her sisters, and her openness to embrace change.

Susan came back to me two weeks later. She had been following her plan for dealing with her sisters, and things were definitely improving. But she had one other important relationship that she wanted to move to a higher plane.

"It's my boyfriend," she said. "I think it's mostly me. I'm just very wary after what happened in my marriage."

"First tell me about your former husband. We never really discussed him before. He seemed to be totally gone from your life."

"My ex? Do you want the long or short version?"

"Let's have the short version for now."

"Well, I met Richard when I was twenty-three and he was thirty-five. And I really fell for him. He was a rebel, and I loved that about him. I was on the rebound from another guy, and I thought Richard was amazing."

"What kind of work did Richard do?"

"He was an auctioneer. But he always had other businesses on the side. He traveled a lot and picked up antiques and bric-a-brac. He also owned a secondhand store where he sold these things. We would go on buying trips together. We would go to a warehouse in New York City that would have boxes for two dollars and four dollars each with all kinds of stuff in them. We would buy ten or twenty boxes and then put these out in his store. It was great fun. We also went to flea markets. And I loved to watch him auction-eering. He had a lot of charisma—a real charmer. But he got in trouble and things changed."

"What did he do?"

"Well, Richard was buddies with a bad group of guys. He got involved with them. They hijacked a truck, and Richard agreed to sell the contents. Unfortunately, the FBI had been tipped and had a film of Richard receiving the merchandise at his store. So he was advised to plead guilty and ask for leniency because he had a pregnant wife who needed him. He kept his mouth shut about the guys, and somehow they got him released from jail after ninety days. But after that Richard was a changed person. He lost his auctioneer's license and also a lot of his self-confidence. He wasn't that spunky, charming guy I fell in love with. After we had our daughter, he seemed to lose interest in us. I'm pretty sure he had affairs, but I never really caught him outright. And then he disappeared, leaving a note saying he was through with us."

"And what about your current boyfriend?"

"Brian? Oh, he's very nice; he's a dentist," she said in a quiet voice.

"You make that sound like a negative."

"No, really. He's a great guy, very steady and very reliable. I can count on him, and that's very important to me. He's really the opposite of Richard in many ways."

"So what's the problem?"

"I'm in love with him, but I'm not sure that I want to spend the rest of my life with him. We don't have a lot of common interests. And there are things that bother me about him. He's stubborn. He spent five years in the military, and he can be very rigid at times. He can be a real steamroller. I won't tolerate that. He's trying to change. He's learning how to relate to me—how to soften his communication. But after Richard, I don't know how much I can trust him to continue to change. Particularly if we were to marry."

"And what is it that you like about him—in addition to his reliability?"

Susan became thoughtful. "He's very kind. He's willing to listen to me. And it's clear that he adores me and wants to marry me. That's a lot, isn't it?"

"That sure is," I responded.

"So what should I do?" she asked.

⇒⟩ *Only you ultimately can decide what's best for you.* ⟨⇐

"No one can tell you what to do about Brian," I said. "For one thing, you're the only one who knows enough about yourself and him to make such a decision. The answer is within you and not me, so you're the one who will have to uncover it. I can help you create the proper framework, though."

"OK," she said. "How do we begin?"

"Begin by looking at your similarities and at your differences. What are some things that Brian loves to do?"

Susan thought for a second. "He loves to invest in real estate. He'll spend hours and hours researching properties."

"OK. Since you have a passion for learning, you might take weekend trips together to communities where he might buy property. You could help him screen communities by learning the demographics of the area and researching property values on the Internet."

"That would be fun! I've already spent time observing different neighborhoods so I've got a head start," Susan noted. "That's definitely something I could see us doing together."

"And I'm sure there are lots of others. Why don't you make a list of the things that Brian loves to do and the things that you love to do. Then brainstorm ideas with Brian for satisfying both of your passions. Challenge yourself to come up with a list of at least twenty activities that you could do together and find joyful and fulfilling."

"All right. But I'm not sure I want to spend that much time with him."

"Of course, there will be lots of times when you'll want to do things separately. Have a separate conversation with Brian about your need for your own space. See if there are any disconnects in how much time each of you thinks is appropriate to spent together and to spend apart."

"That sounds like a good plan," Susan responded. "Believe it or not, we've never discussed these things. It might even be fun!"

"And revealing, too," I added. "You need to remember that each of you has your own masterpiece inside. Ask what you can do to help each other get that masterpiece out into the world. Relish the differences in your strengths, passions, and values, and see how you can support each other in bringing your gift into the world. Great relationships and marriages bring out the best in each partner. There is a reason why opposites do attract!"

Greatness Is Not a Popularity Contest

Michelangelo never really fit in. He stood out from the crowd because of his enormous talent, his personality, and his commitment to his principles.

Many felt he had a chip on his shoulder. More likely, however, he saw what was wrong and spoke out about it. Notice the flattened nose in any painting or statue of Michelangelo. He wasn't born that way. Michelangelo earned it at age fourteen with his inability to keep his mouth shut. When he spotted a drawing error of Pietro Torrigiano, a fellow apprentice at Ghirlandaio's studio, he couldn't help pointing it out. The young artist, angered at Michelangelo's criticism, hauled off and hit him. Torrigiano later described the incident to Benvenuto Cellini, who included it in his autobiography: "Clenching my fist, I gave him such a punch on the nose that I felt the bone and cartilage crush like a biscuit. So that fellow will carry my signature till he dies."

This did not chasten Michelangelo, who continued to call things as he saw them, no matter how disruptive this might be to the established order. Take architecture, for example.

Michelangelo did not consider himself an architect. But once invited into the field, he developed architectural vision, and he would not keep quiet about it. For one thing, he didn't like being patronized by people who didn't share his vision. He generally found himself supervised by a capomaestro who judged his plan and an engineer who supervised the construction. These people, trained in the classical Roman model, were often at odds with Michelangelo's disturbingly innovative designs. Michelangelo fought to be rid of them—not a popular move. He particularly bristled at the supervision of Pope Paul's favorite architect, Antonio da Sangallo. Their arguments grew so fierce that the pope had to silence both of them.

⇛ *To be great, you need to be willing to shake things up.* ⇚

Michelangelo's unwillingness to fit in upset many of among those around him but was also the source of his greatness. For greatness is not a popularity contest. It involves taking risks and shaking things up when necessary. His innovations in architecture were not just disruptive; they revolutionized that art form.

James S. Ackerman, one of America's leading historians of art and architecture, offered this view of Michelangelo's influence:

> Michelangelo, one of the greatest creative geniuses in the history of architecture, frequently claimed he was not an architect. The claim is more than a sculptor's expression of modesty: it is key to the understanding of his buildings, which are conceived as if the masses of a structure were organic forms capable of being moulded and carved, of expressing movement, of forming symphonies of light, shadow and texture, like a statue. . . . This indifference to antique canons shocked Michelangelo's contemporaries, who felt that it was the unique distinction of their age to have revived Roman architecture.

Michelangelo was different; he didn't fit into the mold created by others. His integrity required him to speak out and pursue his vision, no matter what the personal repercussions.

Mark

Mark's résumé stood out from all the rest: he had gotten an Ivy League M.B.A., spent ten years as a manager at a Fortune 500 company, attained progressively more responsible positions in big-name management consulting companies, and been captain of the U.S. Olympic fencing team. Certainly he had the credentials for working with senior-level executives on the consulting project I was staffing. From the way his résumé was written, I could tell that he also had clarity, focus, and determination. The interview confirmed that he was the right person for the job.

That was five years ago. Now Mark, whom I had stayed in touch with after the consulting project was completed with accolades from our client, was looking to start a new business venture. He knew that my primary business now was career coaching. This time he was seeking support for the entrepreneurial challenges he faced.

Mark, an African American, had grown up in the suburbs of a progressive middle-America city during the mid-1960s. His middle-class parents personified their belief that education, integrity, and persistence were critical factors for success in career and in life.

Mark's father, who came from a poor family, had received an athletic scholarship to attend an otherwise all-white school where he was captain of the football and basketball teams. He became the first African American executive in a major office equipment company.

Mark's mother's family, on the other hand, owned a large farm in Missouri and could afford to send her to boarding school. Mark's mother had gone to a fine college in Virginia—rare for an African American woman in those days, even rarer when you consider that she was only fifteen when she started.

Mark tested well enough to get into a program for gifted children that was located in the inner city. He learned that his life was not like that of the African American children he met there. Yes, he had experienced racism on occasion, but he didn't live with the reality that many of these kids faced on a daily basis: gang fights, drugs, alcoholic parents, young single parents, crime, and the stigma of being on welfare.

⇛ *Let what you care about help define you.* ⇚

When Mark, at age ten, was inspired by the popular television series "Zorro" and asked for fencing lessons, his parents readily agreed. There in the city-sponsored sports facility glistening with steel walls and sparkling glass windows, Mark had fun dueling it out with kids from all economic strata, fantasizing himself as a master swordsman and crusading hero. Mark embraced the sport, quickly achieving mastery at junior-level competition.

Mark's exceptional quantitative skills enabled him to attend a special high school program for prospective engineers sponsored by the General Electric Corporation. This opened up the opportunity for him to be accepted by three of the country's leading universities.

He chose an Ivy League school with an outstanding fencing program and a strong African American student community. "Because I was on the fencing team, I was invited by my teammates to be in an elite eating club. I was exposed there to a world that I had never even imagined. F. Scott Fitzgerald had been in this club. There was a certain level of racism because you weren't expected to be there. That was tough. Sometimes I would sit down at a table and no one would talk to me. The chilling was not aggressive. They weren't going to go up to you and insult you, but they weren't going to make you feel at home either. They would just be very happy to ignore you. When I go to reunion events 25 percent are very warm to me, the rest just ignore me. While racism was an endemic part of the social life, it never reached into my academics or my fencing. It never affected my performance. That didn't occur until I went to work for a large corporation.

"After graduating from college," he continued, "I got a job as a systems engineer on the marketing side at one of the top companies in America. Originally, my supervisor was a Chinese man. I did extremely well working for him. After a year and a half I took a leave of absence to earn my M.B.A. at Wharton. It was at my expense, but the company agreed to reinstate me after I got my degree.

"By the time I returned, my former supervisor had left and been replaced by an African American. At first I thought this would be a good thing. But he had certain expectations as to what an African

American's goals and aspirations should be—a certain way that we as African Americans were supposed to behave within the institution. He thought that my expectations were way too aggressive and way too high. He had a very hard time with the fact that I was a national officer of the Society of Black Engineers and that I was still fencing competitively. Also, he thought it absolutely ludicrous that I was exploring the NASA and astronaut programs. Once when we were discussing my career goals, he asked me, 'Are you smoking your lunch?' Not only did he not support me, he thought that I should be penalized for thinking along those lines.

"He moved my best accounts to more senior people, and my fast-track career started to disappear. I was used to creating my own hours as long as I got the job done, which allowed me to do my fencing and have a social life. He told me that unless I adhered strictly to the rules of the organization, I would be fired.

"During this period, I had a lot of self-doubt. I thought that maybe I should just 'play the game' along with all the young, aspiring hot-shots. I spent the next two years trying to conform. I basically just took advantage of what was readily available, kept my mouth shut, and tried to not rock the boat.

"I was on a team servicing a large telecommunications company when I was invited to join the U.S. Olympic fencing team. I was ranked third in the United States at the time. I realized that I couldn't manage the time for both my fencing and my current job. I couldn't look my colleagues in the eye every day and not be carrying my share of the load.

"Also, I understood by that time that I was too outspoken and aggressive for a corporate job and didn't want to continue playing the type of games that I had to play to succeed in that world. I realized that I couldn't be a conformist and retain my personal integrity; it was simply not who I was. So I decided to leave the company."

⋙ *Care for something larger than yourself.* ⋘

In the five years since then, Mark took on a number of consulting jobs that sharpened his marketing skills and provided him with sufficient income to pursue his fencing goals. In fact, he caught the brass ring in fencing when he was selected to captain the U.S. fencing team in Olympic competition. Although he and his team enjoyed success in world competition leading up to the Olympics, he was unable to participate in the Olympic Games due to an injury. Mark was devastated but remained with the team, rooting his teammates on.

Sitting there in my office, I saw that he hadn't added an ounce of fat to his trim physique since I had last seen him five years before. I mentioned that to him. "I still fence competitively, jog regularly, watch what I eat, and meditate. Fencing is one of the best workouts for a short period of time you can possibly have." Mark would never miss a chance to promote the sport that he loved.

Mark got to the point of the meeting. "I want to start a TV production company that promotes the sport of fencing in the United States and raise awareness for the sport. And I want to provide a place for disadvantaged youths to have a place to experience what I did as a child."

My first thought was that he was going to have an uphill battle— make that uphill over a ten-story-high wall. Fencing in the United States doesn't have the cachet that it does in some European countries. The sport had gotten about as much TV coverage during the past Summer Games as curling does during the Winter Games. I also thought about the huge losses that promoters of the professional soccer league and the XFL football league had incurred, despite having extensive media coverage and investors with deep pockets. As a coach, I had an agenda to help Mark achieve his dream, and that included playing devil's advocate to determine Mark's level of commitment.

I asked, "Why are you so passionate about fencing?"

Mark replied, "I enjoy the martial arts aspect, and it's something I excelled in, but it's also the people, the training, and the discipline."

I probed further. "What is the feeling you get when you are in a match?"

Mark was clear in his response. "It's a combination of knowing that you have a plan; that you have an opponent who is committed to thwart your plan at all costs; and when you are able to execute despite the opposition, you will achieve success."

I asked him what his business mission was. He replied, "I want to introduce more African Americans to this sport and make it as popular in the African American community as other martial arts are, like karate. I know that if it wasn't for the leaders who came before me, I would not have had the opportunities that I have had in my life. I feel it's very important that I give back as much as I can— to help create new economic engines within the African American community and also create new opportunities. I want to pass on the opportunities and experiences I've had through fencing."

"So what's it going to take to achieve your dream?" I asked.

Mark answered, "I have to keep things in perspective. I'm trying to build an industry that doesn't exist, with a population base that is neither large nor well understood, with my limited financial resources. On the other hand, over the last fifty years other activities including martial arts, popular elsewhere, have exploded here in the United States. Consider amateur soccer, karate, tai-chi, yoga. None of these had a significant constituency here fifty years ago. My vision is very clear. I really believe in what I'm doing, and once the systems and structures I'm working on are in place, I believe that I can have an explosive positive impact. That motivates me and keeps me in the game."

Mark had been working hard over the past year to develop business and marketing plans for his new enterprise. Technology was important in producing high-quality fencing broadcasts so that the action, often too fast for the eye to discern, could be recorded and played back in super-slow motion. This technology was expensive. So were the staff and consultants needed to do the editing, the promotional literature, the press releases, and the myriad jobs needed to build a production company. And there was the state-of-the-art website to deliver streaming video, an online store for fencing equipment and related items, and the fencing schools for inner-city youth.

Mark won me over with his steely determination, clarity of vision, understanding of the risks, ability to sell the benefits, and superb qualifications to make it happen. If he could enroll me in his vision for promoting fencing in the United States, perhaps he could enroll others—sponsors and investors. He would need all of his physical stamina, Ivy League education, discipline, life values, family's support, skill at creating and nurturing relations, and unwavering commitment to success for the journey ahead.

*Follow your principles,
no matter how difficult or inconvenient.*

Another year has gone by. Mark is now a man on a mission. He gets people's attention with the strength of his vision, his intelligence, and his energy. He has put a substantial part of his own wealth into his new venture and has convinced other investors to share his dream. And he has convinced a lot of people that it is now fencing's turn to capture the attention of people who are into sports and personal development.

Maybe Mark is ahead of his time, like Michelangelo when he broke the mold with his unusual and controversial architectural designs. But maybe, like Michelangelo, with perseverance, a willingness to take risks, and an unyielding commitment to succeed, Mark can find a way to achieve his vision. Maybe it is fencing's turn.

But whether he succeeds in his fencing venture or not, Mark has remained true to himself. Mark has not just followed the easy route but has created a life that fits him, and he has followed his principles no matter how difficult or inconvenient. He may or may not achieve the success of Michelangelo, but like Michelangelo he has lived with integrity. In this regard he has created a masterpiece.

Sculpt Your Personal Masterpiece

Michelangelo lived a life that fit him—and did so from an early age. He discovered his talent of drawing, the hand obedient to the mind, as a young child. As a teenager, he uncovered his lifelong passion for sculpting. And his value of glorifying God and God's works came from his family and the society of Renaissance Italy where the Roman Catholic Church prevailed. He found a way of uniting his values, passions, and strengths by creating wondrous sculptures, like his three *Pietàs*, dedicated to the greater glory of his God, and the *David*, glorifying that greatest of God's works, humankind. Michelangelo was true to his principles throughout his long and productive life. Michelangelo lived a life of integrity.

For most of us, the process of discovering and pursuing a life of integrity is more complicated. Our lives are fast paced and confused and don't readily fit together. Susan had the challenge of transforming her relationships with her sisters and her boyfriend while maintaining her central value of authenticity. Mark had to break free of his life as an "organization man" in corporate America to be himself and to pursue his dream of helping to promote and expand the sport of fencing.

The journey to integrity is often tortuous and difficult. We might even fail. But when you think about, isn't that journey worth taking?

As you embark on this journey, ask yourself the following questions:

+ Who are the people I most respect?

+ How do they behave in all areas of their lives, not just in their careers?

+ Do I ever sacrifice my values and passions for the sake of convenience?

+ Am I living the life that fits me, or am I living out other people's expectations?

+ Do I do what I am passionate about every day?

+ Am I making a difference to my family and friends?

+ Am I making a difference in the lives of others?

+ Am I authentic? Do others know me as I truly am, or do they see a mask that disguises my authentic self?

+ Do I always honor my word?

+ Do I take full responsibility for all areas of my life?

+ Am I open to new possibilities for my own growth and development?

Discovery Exercises

1. Refer back to your discovery exercises for Chapters 1 and 2, where you uncovered your values, passions, and strengths. Write down your two highest values, your two strongest passions, and your two greatest strengths. Leave ten lines between each.

2. Beneath each of these six items, write an evaluation of how great a role it plays in your current life. The greater the role, the more you are living a life that fits you—that is, a life of integrity.

3. Under each of these evaluations, write three ways in which you could increase the extent of involvement of these values, passions, and strengths in your life.

4. Develop lists for daily, weekly, monthly, and annual habits that you commit to practicing to nurture your body, heart, and mind so as to ensure that you are living a life of integrity. For example, meditate and exercise daily, go on weekly outings with your family or friends, participate in a new culture-enhancing activity monthly, and get annual medical checkups. Create and schedule opportunities to do what you love, satisfy your values, and develop your talents.

5. Now incorporate these changes into your daily living. You can never have too much integrity!

Rondanini Pietà

Michelangelo worked on this *Pietà* until a few days before his death at the age of eighty-nine. Considered by many to be Michelangelo's most poignant work, the Blessed Virgin and Son appear to be fused together so that we can no longer distinguish who is carrying whom.

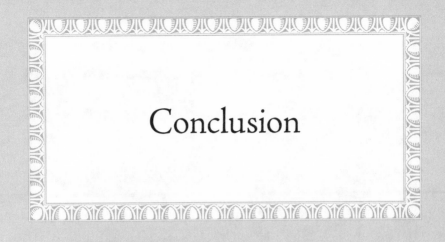

Conclusion

There is an art to mastery. And there is an art to making changes in your life. Understand that, and you've taken the first step toward your masterpiece—the extraordinary life you've always wanted.

To practice the art of change means to persevere with purpose. Like turning marble into a masterpiece, turning your passions, values, and talents into an extraordinary life requires a unique combination of creativity, strategy, and faith. You must harness your deepest insight and then direct it out toward your goal.

As we've seen, the life of Michelangelo holds powerful lessons in the art of personal mastery. And we've seen how people's lives can change by applying the Michelangelo Method to the pursuit of their personal masterpiece.

Yours can, too.

By following the Michelangelo Method, you can release your inner masterpiece and create an extraordinary life. After all, the potential for mastery is inside each and every one of us.

So use this method. Find your vision. Commit to it. Plan, prepare, innovate, and fight. Take on your Goliath. Create your masterpiece.

The proof is in the doing.

Creation of Man from the Sistine Chapel
Michelangelo chose as the centerpiece for his great Sistine
Chapel masterpiece the precise moment when God awak-
ened man into his image. This was the moment of creation,
when Adam receives the gift of life and all the blessings that
God bestows upon humankind.

The Granger Collection, New York

Epilogue

What happens when people like you and I put all the principles of the Michelangelo Method into practice? The story of Roger and Adam, two colleagues who take this journey, epitomizes how to release your inner masterpiece and create an extraordinary life.

Roger and Adam

Roger Avery was an original, the sort of man who, when he was walking out the door of the office for the last time, clicked his heels as he crossed down the row of cubicles, a Gene Kelly in Dockers.

In leaving in that way, Roger Avery became a mythic figure in his office, the projection of everyone's fantasies of getting out. For he had gotten out—clicking his heels even—and they had simply watched the scene from over the cubicle walls.

It was fifteen years ago when Roger and his colleague Adam Green had started working together in the accounting department of a large semiconductor manufacturer. They were always on separate projects and were never competing for the same promotion, so they became easy friends, office friends, friends who'd have lunch in the basement cafeteria.

Roger and Adam were different in many ways. But they appreciated each other's differences and looked forward to shooting the breeze—and complaining.

When they first met, Roger and Adam had only been working in the accounting department for about a year. Back then, they were enthusiastic and hungry for challenges. They were young. They were at the start of what they thought to be exciting careers in finance. They would mold the future with the will of their hands and hearts.

When they both hit twenty-seven the same week, after the office carolers compressed their names into a tortured rendition of "Happy Birthday," they discussed this future over the sad remnants of a requisite chocolate layer cake. One day they'd change the way this company ran. They'd institute new procedures. They'd implement new management technologies. One day they'd run this department. One day they'd be competing for the chief financial officer's job.

But as time went on, Roger and Adam both became frustrated with office politics. They learned quickly that significant promotions in the company were few and far between, and even when they were available they were usually offered to people outside the company. Without new challenges, work became drudgery.

At the same time, the job market seemed too depressing to consider. And what would they consider anyway? They knew they didn't want this job, but what would they do if they weren't doing this? And what could be better than this—as bad as this might be? They were conflicted. On one hand, they were resigned. On the other hand, they held out for the cinematic fantasy: an escape route hidden behind the poster on the prison wall.

The light illuminating their lunchtime conversations became more focused on their dreams, their hobbies, their lives outside the office walls. Adam would share with Roger his love of photography, the artistic photographs he had taken in the Pacific Northwest, and his passion for Italian art, particularly Michelangelo's magnificent frescoes on the ceiling of the Sistine Chapel. Roger would share with Adam his love of sailing, the weekend's forecast for easterly winds, the picture of the house he rented on the harbor line. One day he even produced a smudged sketch on a paper napkin of what he proclaimed was the "ultimate sailing machine."

Yes, they wondered aloud how they could change their lives, how they might turn them inside out and somehow make their weekend passions their daily work, and yet the world of change seemed a distant speck at the end of this universe, a phantom planet.

For Adam, the energy required to risk change was not there. When he looked at his life, he saw commitments. Family and community responsibilities. These were choices he had made years before. There was stability in these choices, a foundation of love that he wouldn't trade for the mist of a dream.

But Roger's life had a long and tremorous fault that would eventually shake it to its core.

Roger discovered his wife had begun drinking again after seven years of sobriety. He tried to keep both her and their marriage together. Deep down he sensed the world was crumbling too fast for his loving hands to hold. When he discovered she was having an affair, he knew the spaces had grown so wide they could never be closed.

On their sixth anniversary, Roger and his wife found themselves without candlelight. Instead, a divorce deposition lay between them in the glare of a harsh spotlight that focused on everything they'd done wrong. When that light turned on Roger, he was forced to look deep inside himself. There, a word jabbed at his heart, prodding him, whispering again and again, a single word: *change.*

Soon "change" became Roger's mantra. Each day at lunch Roger's daily news became his daily revelation. One weekend he moved into a condo. The next, he sold his almost new BMW and bought a used Toyota to save money. He talked about getting out to do "something" he still wasn't sure of. Six months later, there was Roger Avery leaving the office, clicking his heels, dancing out the door, and dropping off the radar.

When Roger disappeared from their gray universe, rumors bounced off all the office walls. Some of them seemed reasonable enough. Roger was working for the competition. Roger was going to Columbia to get his M.B.A. Someone thought they saw Roger teaching market analytics at the community college. Others were less than reasonable. Roger retired in Costa Rica and was living on the beach, watching toucans, and eating papaya from the trees. Roger had found God and joined a cult in Montana. One guy even suggested that Roger was secretly working for the CIA in the mountains of Pakistan.

When Adam got a call from Roger three years after his departure, the mystery remained. Roger was nothing less than cryptic. There was no small talk. Adam's "how have you beens?" were answered with a simple laugh and "that story is best told in person." And when Adam hung up the phone, agreeing to lunch with him at his home two hours away, he was a bit apprehensive.

Adam was afraid of what he might come face-to-face with. Would he see Roger the madman, the schoolteacher, the beach bum, or the government double agent?

The drive to Roger's home took Adam to the waterfront of a small, picturesque mill town that had become a destination for weekenders. Roger's new home turned out to be a converted warehouse on the harbor. When Adam stepped out of the car, the salt breeze wafted over him. He felt instantly calmed. Something about this place felt right. This was exactly where Roger belonged.

Roger, with a relaxed smile, let Adam into his home. His hair was a little longer than Adam remembered—and a little grayer on the edges—and his face wore not the ragged lines of age but the crinkles of life. He took Adam's extended hand and gave him a hug and a tour of the house.

Every inch of the home said Roger Avery, from the hardwood floors to the rudder on the wall, to the open kitchen, to the artfully worn leather chair that sat before the large bay window—the perfect vantage point to view the water.

And when Adam looked out the bay window to the water, his mouth dropped open. Sitting in the harbor tied to the dock was something he had once seen etched on a crumpled napkin, the "ultimate sailing machine," the sailboat Roger had conceived so many years ago.

"That's your boat!" Adam exclaimed.

Roger nodded and smiled. "The Ultimate Sailing Machine. That's what I'm doing these days. Right now, around the world, there are thirty-five of these babies on the water."

Adam was dumbstruck. Roger hadn't just left their office. He had left his old life completely. And he had no reason to look back. He had a home that was nothing less than a sanctuary. He had a new career. He had started his own business on a dream, and now he was thriving.

All that aside, what struck Adam most about Roger was the look on his face. It was a bemused look, the look of a man who almost couldn't believe his good fortune. In short, Roger Avery was happy, ecstatic even. He had started again—this time on the right foot.

But what had turned his life around? When Adam last saw Roger three years ago, sitting over their respective lunches, discussing their respective frustrations, Roger's life was far worse than Adam's. Yet Roger Avery now appeared to be a butterfly released from the cocoon. Watching him here, you could never believe that he had once spent time on the ground.

"OK, Roger. How did you do it?" Adam asked. "How did you get from where we were together to here?"

Roger related his experience with a career coach, who had helped him realize that the extraordinary life he was seeking was already inside him. He and his coach then uncovered his highest values, passions, and talents and chipped away at the personal and professional issues that were obscuring what his coach described as "the masterpiece within."

Adam was impressed. But deep inside he felt that he was too committed to the path he had chosen long ago. "Sometimes," he thought, "you just have to lie in the bed you've made for yourself. Sometimes you just have to stop making choices."

But Adam was wrong. For to live is to choose. What is life but a string of choices? With each passing second, life unfolds possibilities. In the course of living and breathing, we choose one possibility over another. Sometimes in choosing we are cautious, sometimes we are bold; but however we choose, in choosing, we open ourselves to another choice.

You might say each choice opens us up to another life. Like a series of Russian dolls, within each choice another self hides. Nested inside each choice is a path that's revealed only if you have embraced that particular possibility.

Our smallest choices can have profound effects on our world. Choosing paper over plastic might save the world—especially if enough of us do it. The simple flap of a butterfly's wings could set in motion a chain of events ultimately causing a tornado thousands of miles away.

Adam Green was twenty years old when the most important choice of his life was before him. The choice: stay at his fraternity party and have one more beer with the boys, or go home and go to sleep. He chose one more beer.

And nothing terrible happened as a result of that beer. He did not get into an accident. He did not even wake up with the hint of a hangover. He did, however, end up staying out later than he had expected. An hour later.

When he returned home to his dorm room, he slipped out of his clothes, slipped into bed, and closed his eyes. It wasn't even 1 A.M.

The next morning he awoke peacefully. Sunlight streamed through the blinds. The thwack of a soccer ball on the lawn below beat out a playful cadence. Someone laughed outside the window. His finger pulled down the metal blinds. It was a beautiful spring afternoon.

It was afternoon!

Adam pulled himself from the window and back to bed where he checked his alarm clock. It was 1 P.M. He shook the clock in disgust. Why hadn't it gone off? Because the button to set it hadn't been pressed.

Somehow, inexplicably, his choice to stay up just a tiny bit later had disturbed his routine, and in short, he screwed up. He had missed his presentation for his photography class final project.

In the end, the choice to stay and have that one more beer led to a chain of events that began with the missed presentation and ended with him changing majors yet again, this time from photography to business administration. In a way, you might say that one more beer made Adam Green the man he is today.

Google the name "Adam Green" and you'll find about 880,000 mentions. Thousands of possible lives to have lived: a young folk musician; at least fifteen lawyers, two of whom work together; one CEO of a multimillion-dollar corporation; someone who ran the New York City Marathon in under three hours in 2002; a soccer player of some note; an accomplished film director; an archivist at a museum; a scientist who conducts studies in the field of analogical reasoning; a handful of psychotherapists both here and abroad; and one accountant at a semiconductor firm who years later still worked in the same gray cubicle, in the same gray office. Thousands of different Adam Greens; at least a million choices that made them the Adam Greens they are today.

And if they're not the Adam Green they wanted to be, well, it's because of the choices they made. They'll just have to live with their choices and make the best of their time on this planet as an Adam Green.

But wouldn't it be nice to think that some days they could switch places? What if Adam Green the banker called up Adam Green the musician and they agreed, if only for one night, to play the other's hand?

One Adam Green would teach the other a few songs on the guitar, and one Adam Green would teach the other all about compound interest rates. Adam Green the banker would race up to the stage that night and receive the fans' adoration, and that night Adam Green the musician would go to dinner with a client and dine on steak and Bordeaux wine. And then, the next day, Adam Green and Adam Green would return to their old lives—or not.

Some people might say the choice to be someone else isn't ever available, except in some Hollywood film where mother becomes daughter or son becomes father and they learn to understand one another. Face facts. Adam Green is Adam Green. We are who we are. Sometimes you just don't have the choice to change.

Somewhere Roger Avery disagreed. "What would have happened if Michelangelo chose to continue his traditional studies and didn't persuade his father to allow him to apprentice with Ghirlandaio? Would he have become a successful merchant? Would he have ever dined with the Medici?

"And what about his homeland? Would he have gone on to lead the defense of Florence? Or would Michelangelo have been just another casualty of war? Would Florentine society have crumbled without the *David* to inspire its citizens?

"And what would have happened to art? Would someone else have applied his genius to understanding how important structural anatomy is to drawing the human form? Would someone else take this knowledge and create the dome of St. Peter's Basilica? Would there have been a Rodin if Michelangelo the future merchant had chosen not to be Michelangelo the artist?

And would there be a Roger Avery?

A number of years back Roger Avery made a choice to become a different Roger Avery. He chose to leave his firm. He chose to radically change his life. He found his vision, and he chose to bring it out from the stone.

Years later, Roger chose to find out what had become of his old friend, Adam Green. Roger dialed Adam's old telephone number. Just like Adam, it had not changed.

Adam thought, "Maybe tomorrow I'll give Roger Avery a call and ask him a question. What if I had chosen to be Adam Green the photographer?" He already knew that his answer would be another question: "What if you chose to be one now?"

That night, Adam found himself thinking of the first photograph he ever took. He had begged his father for a camera when he was just eleven years old.

When Adam opened his gifts on his twelfth birthday, there it was inside a blue box wrapped with baseball bat wrapping paper. His very own Brownie! He had no time for other toys. He wasted little time playing with the football or the model train with the real steam engine. He studied the manual, loaded the camera, and rushed to take his first picture.

But what to take? He raced around the house, camera in hand. Nothing seemed interesting enough. He had seen everything a hundred times in that house. He wanted his first picture to be something new, something he had never really looked at before.

When he was searching the house, he passed by the mirror in his bathroom. He caught himself reflected backward as a mirror does. Backward! That was it. There was only one thing in the house that he had never seen as it truly was: himself.

He turned the camera on himself, guessing at the angle and hoping that he would still be in focus a mere arm's length away.

When his father brought his first roll of film back from the photo store, he rushed to find that picture. There it was. The image shot blurry. The composition askew. The work immature. But there he was.

For the first time, he saw himself as others saw him. He *saw* himself. He must have stared at that picture a thousand times.

Adam wondered where that photo ended up. Did it fall between the floorboards when he had moved upstate? Did his mother just forget to pack it? Did his brother tear it in a rage when they fought over a girl whose name he could scarcely remember? Whatever happened he had lost it forever—except in his mind's eye.

It was past midnight. Adam padded quietly around the house. His daughter slept soundly in her bedroom, still hugging the pink bunny he had given to her when she was just three. Down the hall, his wife smiled in her sleep. Was she dreaming that he had come to bed? He'd like to think so. The rest of the house was dark, but he knew it well. Each room built by the work he had done in this life—except the basement. It remained a square of cinderblocks, in it a few shelves of disorganized storage.

He rummaged through the shelves of boxes. He found it there behind some old tax receipts. His old Brownie. He clicked the shutter. Film printed inside the camera. He turned the knob. Somehow—is it possible—the camera was loaded.

From the corner of his eye, he caught his reflection in an old mirror. The graying hair, the slight paunch, the lines of regret—he was older now, but you can never be too old to choose, as long as you're still alive.

Adam mounted the camera on the shelf, pulling the mirror beside him. He stood before it, looking at himself. He thought of Roger Avery and how if Roger could see him now he might click his heels. He thought of Michelangelo. Of his Adam in the Sistine Chapel and the space between Adam's finger and that of God's. Of events unleashed when their fingers met, all choice, all life, all possibility, the flowering of genius, and the masterpieces not yet made.

This is Adam's finger reaching out to the mirror. This is Adam Green reaching out to Adam Green. This is Adam releasing the shutter. This is his first photograph.

This is his creation.

Appendix A

Sample Values, Passions, and Strengths

The following sample lists are provided to assist you in discovering your own values, passions, and strengths. Add your own unique values, passions, and strengths as needed.

Sample Personal Values

Achievement	Adventure	Authenticity
Beauty	Compassion	Competition
Cooperation	Creativity	Equality
Family	Freedom	Friendship
Happiness	Harmony	Health
Integrity	Knowledge	Love
Loyalty	Openness	Relationships
Religion	Reputation	Romance
Self-actualization	Self-respect	Social relationships
Spirituality	Wealth	Work-life balance

Sample Career Values

Accountability	Can-do mind-set	Compassion
Competition	Creativity	Equality
Excellence	Flexibility	Formality
Honesty	Innovation	Integrity
Knowledge	Leadership	Loyalty

Openness

Seniority

Volunteerism

Reputation

Social relationships

Wealth

Self-reliance

Teamwork

Work-life balance

Sample Passions

Racing
motorcycles

Photography

Crossword puzzles

Gardening

Restoring old
automobiles

Playing poker

Stand-up comedy

Playing with
model trains

Helping the
homeless

Designing websites

Painting
landscapes

Crafting

Planning family
gatherings

Playing board
games

Getting together
with friends

Tennis

Performing magic
tricks

Running
marathons

Working with
animals

Renovating homes

Genealogy

Organic cooking

Scuba diving

Geotrekking

Coaching youth
baseball

Raising funds
for charities

Piloting planes

Teaching adult
ed classes

Listening to
classical music

Interior decorating

Singing with a
choral group

Scouting

Breeding dogs

Spending week-
ends at a bed-
and-breakfast

Teaching art
to children

Preserving the
environment

Collecting stamps

Golfing

Sailing

Acting in community
theater

Traveling to national
parks

Hiking

Writing for health
magazines

Studying military
history

Writing book
reviews

Debating

Reading self-help
books

Being a volunteer
firefighter

Handicapping horse
races

Going to movies

Sample Strengths

Acting	Administrative abilities	Analytic skills
Working with animals	Athletic ability	Gardening
Communications skills	Computer skills	Carpentry
Cooking	Storytelling	Construction
Dancing	Creative writing	Teaching
Dexterity	Debating	Creativity
Following directions	Diplomacy	Design
Imagination	Working with children	Endurance
Artistic ability	Interpersonal relations	Healing
Investigation	Leadership	Singing
Listening	Managing people	Interviewing
Memorization	Navigation	Research
Networking	Observation	Learning new things
Perceptiveness	Persistence	Marketing
Playing a musical instrument	Physical strength	Negotiation
	Public speaking	Organizational skills
		Persuasiveness
		Planning
		Photography

Appendix B

Resources to Support You

Here is a list of books and websites that we recommend for additional information and insights to support you in career change, career mastery, business start-up, and personal development. We invite you to visit our website, michelangelomethod.com, to get the latest additions to our list of resources.

Career Change

+ *The Pathfinder* by Nicholas Lore. A practical guide for finding more fulfilling and engaging work.

+ *I Could Do Anything If I Only Knew What It Was* by Barbara Sher. Valuable insights to help you create a vision for your future career.

+ *The Purpose of Your Life: Finding Your Place in the World Using Synchronicity, Intuition, and Uncommon Sense* by Carol Adrienne and James Redfield. An inspiring and valuable guide for discovering your purpose in life.

+ *What Color Is Your Parachute? 2007: A Practical Manual for Job-Hunters and Career-Changers* by Richard Nelson Bolles. A guide that addresses the nuts and bolts of changing jobs and careers.

+ wetfeet.com. A great website for investigating potential careers.

+ careers.org. Resources on alternative work.

+ thefutureofwork.net. Valuable insights about how globalization, technology, and other trends are changing the nature of work.

Career Success and Mastery (General)

+ *The Inner Game of Work: Focus, Learning, Pleasure, and Mobility in the Workplace* by W. Timothy Gallwey. A refreshingly new way to think about your work and career and how to improve your performance.

+ *Overcoming Your Strengths: 8 Reasons Why Successful People Derail and How to Remain on Track* by Lois P. Frankel. A unique approach for keeping your career on track. Provides great advice on how to be successful in your current job and develop the skills for your next job.

+ *First, Break All the Rules: What the World's Greatest Managers Do Differently* by Marcus Buckingham and Curt Coffman. What every manager and leader should know about keeping employees engaged in their work.

+ *The 4 Realities of Success During and After College* by Bob Roth. A primer for college students about to enter the workforce. Provides practical advice on conducting a job search and getting off to a great start in your new career.

+ *Power Networking Second Edition: 59 Secrets for Personal & Professional Success* by Donna Fisher and Sandy Vilas. Information from two master networkers on how to take your networking skills—among the most important skills for changing careers and achieving career success—to the next level.

Career Success and Mastery (Specific Careers)

+ *Manage IT: A Step by Step Guide to Help New and Aspiring IT Managers Make the Right Career Choices and Gain the Skills Necessary* by Joe Santana and Jim Donovan. A practical guide to support new information technology managers make the transition from technical professional to effective manager.

+ *Million Dollar Consulting, New and Updated Edition: The Professional's Guide to Growing a Practice* by Alan Weiss. Valuable insights into building a successful consultancy, for both beginning and experienced consultants.

Entrepreneurship and Business

+ *The E-Myth Revisited: Why Most Small Businesses Don't Work and What to Do About It* by Michael E. Gerber. Key distinctions and strategies that will help you make the transition from employee to small business owner.

+ *Managing the Professional Service Firm* by David H. Maister. A comprehensive how-to guide on building and managing a professional services firm.

+ *Nichecraft: Using Your Specialness to Focus Your Business, Corner Your Market and Make Customers Seek You Out* by Lynda Falkenstein. Information on defining and focusing on your target market.

+ sba.gov/starting (Small Business Administration website). Resources on starting and running a small business.

Personal Development

- *The Art of Possibility* by Rosamund Stone Zander and Benjamin Zander. Inspirational teachings on how to lead a life of infinite possibility.

- *The 7 Habits of Highly Effective People* by Stephen R. Covey. Guide to seven habits to be practiced regularly in order to improve business and personal relationships.

Books About Michelangelo

Pope John Paul II, in a 2002 poem, urged the cardinals who would choose the next pope to take inspiration from Michelangelo—the nine biblical scenes from the book of Genesis on the ceiling and *The Last Judgment* on the altar wall of the Sistine Chapel. The pope wrote the following:

> It is here, beneath this wondrous Sistine profusion of color that the cardinals assemble—the community responsible for the legacy of the keys of the Kingdom.
>
> During the conclave Michelangelo must teach them. Do not forget: all things are naked and opened before His [God's] eyes. You who see all, point to him! He will point him out.

We recommend the following books about Michelangelo's art and his life, which might inspire you as they did the conclave of cardinals who elected Pope Benedict XVI.

- *The Agony and the Ecstasy: A Biographical Novel of Michelangelo* by Irving Stone. This fascinating, very well-researched biographical novel reads like fiction.

+ *Michelangelo: The Sistine Chapel Ceiling: Illustrations, Introductory Essay, Backgrounds and Sources, Critical Essays* (Norton Critical Studies in Art History) by Charles Seymour (editor). This title offers a full description of the dual drama—artistic and spiritual—posed to Michelangelo by the ceiling of the Sistine Chapel.

+ *Michelangelo: A Biography* by George Bull. Bull's is possibly the best Michelangelo biography available—complete and very readable.

+ *The Life of Michelangelo* by Ascanio Condivi, Hellmut Wohl (editor), and Alice Sedgwick Wohl (translator). Condivi, a pupil, assistant, and confidante of Michelangelo, provides a contemporary view, often using his own firsthand experience.

+ *Complete Poems and Selected Letters of Michelangelo* by Michelangelo and Creighton Gilbert (translator). A great way to understand Michelangelo's character, values, and relationships is through these poems and letters.

+ *Michelangelo* by Anthony Hughes. Using beautiful, full-color pictures of Michelangelo's work, Hughes makes it easy to follow the parallel progression of Michelangelo's life and art.

+ *Life of Michelangelo* by Giorgio Vasari (Introduction by Frank Sadowski; translation by Gaston Du C. De Vere). Full of opinions and easily read, this biography by Vasari, an art historian who knew Michelangelo, is a primary source for all modern biographies.

Appendix C

Career and Life Coaching Services to Support and Guide You

We hope that reading this book has provided new information and insights on how to release your masterpiece, as well as the inspiration to begin your own journey to an extraordinary career and life. We selected stories of coaching clients that represent a diversity of goals sought and roadblocks encountered. But your journey is unique, as is the support you might need along the way. A personal coach can help you discover your masterpiece, keep your focus on creating your extraordinary life when your ordinary life overwhelms you, challenge you to innovate and push your limits, celebrate your victories, and connect you with resources to reach your goals faster and better than you could alone.

Our coaching company, Career Renaissance LLC, provides highly experienced coaches who are trained and certified in the Michelangelo Method. We are available for individual coaching and have an international network of coaches with varied career and life experience. We invite you to contact us to connect you with the best coach to help you release your inner masterpiece. You can contact us at info@michelangelomethod.com or (201) 405-0973; or visit us at our website: michelangelomethod.com.

In addition to personal coaching services, we offer corporate executive coaching, mentor coaching for new or experienced coaches, workshops and seminars, presentations and keynote speeches, individual and group assessments, corporate outplacement services, and Michelangelo Method tours and retreats. Contact us for more information about these services.

Bibliography

Ackerman, James. *The Architecture of Michelangelo*. Chicago, 1961.

Beck, James. *Three Worlds of Michelangelo*. New York, 1999.

Bull, George. *Michelangelo, a Biography*. New York, 1995.

Bull, George. *Michelangelo: Life, Letters, and Poetry*. Oxford, 1987.

Condivi, Ascanio. *The Life of Michelangelo*, translated by Alice Wohl. University Park, PA, 1999.

Hall, James. *Michelangelo and the Reinvention of the Human Body*. New York, 2005.

Hibbard, Howard. *Michelangelo*. New York, 1974.

Hughes, Anthony. *Michelangelo*. London and New York, 1997.

King, Ross. *Michelangelo & the Pope's Ceiling*. London, 2003.

Linscott, Robert (ed.). *Complete Poems and Selected Letters of Michelangelo*. Princeton, 1963.

Murray, Linda. *Michelangelo*. London, 1980.

Scigliano, Eric. *Michelangelo's Mountain*. New York, 2005.

Seymour, Charles, Jr. *Michelangelo: The Sistine Chapel Ceiling*. New York, 1972.

Stone, Irving. *The Story of Michelangelo's Pietà*. Garden City, NY, 1964.

Symonds, John Addington. *The Life of Michelangelo Buonarroti*. New York, 1936.

Vasari, Giorgio. *Life of Michelangelo* (1568), translated by Gaston de Vere. New York, 2003.

Wallace, William (ed.). *Michelangelo: Selected Readings*. New York and London, 1999.

Index

About the Authors

Kenneth Schuman is cofounder of Career Renaissance LLC. He provides career and life coaching for individuals and groups seeking new and better paths. Ken previously earned an M.B.A. from Columbia University and an M.S.W. from Hunter College. He is certified by Target Training International as a professional behavioral and values analyst. Ken has been executive director of the Queens County Mental Health Society and the Lower East Side Family Union. He worked as assistant to the mayor of New York City, which ultimately led to his appointment as commissioner for economic development. Ken next moved into investment banking as vice president of corporate finance for Lehman Brothers and then into development of housing for low- and moderate-income families. He lives with his wife, Wendy, in Essex Fells, New Jersey.

Ronald Paxton is cofounder of Career Renaissance LLC. He specializes in career and life coaching and has conducted workshops and seminars internationally. Ron was formerly president of the New Jersey Professional Coaches Association and is a board member of the Northern New Jersey Chapter of the American Society of Training and Development. He is the host of Coach U Career Coaches and Information Technology Coaches Special Interest Groups. Previously he held management and executive positions at IBM, Unisys, and PricewaterhouseCoopers. Ron is certified by Target Training International as a professional behavioral and values analyst. He is a graduate of Coach U and has a master of science degree from New York University. Ron lives with his wife, Nancy, in Oakland, New Jersey.